MW01631699

Look Me In the Eye

Using Video to Build Relationships with Customers, Partners and Teams

JULIE HANSEN

ISBN: 978-1-7375037-0-5

PRAISE FOR
LOOK ME IN THE EYE

"If you're not striving for virtual excellence, you'll be left behind in a digital or hybrid future. Julie Hansen shares insider secrets from on-camera professionals and hundreds of helpful tips for building deeper relationships and engaging customers on video."

Steffen Sajonz, Global VP Sales & GTM Program Office, SAP

"Virtual selling is a highly competitive and increasingly difficult arena in which to differentiate, be heard, and connect with others. Julie Hansen goes well beyond the basics and provides a roadmap to building relationships on video that drive sales."

Jill Konrath, Author, *SNAP Selling & More Sales Less Time*

"I'll never look at my webcam the same way again! Practical, directly actionable, and often surprising, Look Me In The Eye has me sitting straighter, engaging more effectively, and communicating more successfully over the web."

Peter Cohan, Author, *Great Demo!*

"Julie's style of writing is easy to consume and makes even difficult concepts easily understandable. This is an excellent book, but my favorite chapters concern "cheats" and video body language which is completely different from live interaction. Excellent insight. Julie shows you how to make the camera work for you. This book will be required reading for my entire sales staff. And remember- the camera is your friend!

Dave Salinas, Director of Sales North America, Givaudan

"In the future, will you be spending more time on camera or less? The honest and obvious answer is more, so we can't just show up. We must be intentional. What Julie provides here is expert advice – some of it counterintuitive, much of it overlooked, and all of it practical – to help you connect with people in more meaningful and memorable ways."

Ethan Beute, Chief Evangelist, BombBomb
Co-author, *Rehumanize Your Business and Human-Centered Communication*

DEDICATION

To all the salespeople, business leaders, and entrepreneurs who never set out for a life on camera, may this book make your journey more enjoyable and more rewarding in every way.

CONTENTS

A FEW NOTES FROM THE AUTHOR

This Book is for Anyone Who Wants to Improve Their Relationships on Video.

If you desire to communicate and connect with others more successfully on video, this book is for you. While I use examples from sales throughout the book, executives, speakers, entrepreneurs and others will find the techniques and skills in these pages equally effective for building new relationships and strengthening existing ones, so don't get hung up on terminology. *(P.S. If you communicate with a desire to connect, influence, and achieve results, you just might be a salesperson!)*

This Book Is for Those Doing Live Video Calls, Meetings, and or Pre-Recorded Videos.

The techniques you'll learn in this book work beautifully whether you're talking to a live person on the other side of the screen (**synchronous** video) or recording a video to send to someone to watch at their convenience (**asynchronous** video). Synchronous and asynchronous are pretty sterile words for a conversation between two or more people, so I'll be referring to them as either live video calls and meetings or pre-recorded videos. Most of the examples and suggestions will be for live video; however, I will point out the tactical differences for pre-recorded video where applicable.

This Book Is Not About Technology.

It's about helping you build a deeper, more meaningful relationship with your audience leading to more sales, improved collaboration, and greater productivity. You can build a relationship using a free platform, a fifty-dollar camera, and the light from your kitchen window, and you can lose a relationship with a set-up suitable for an

Apple product launch. Technology only provides you with the potential to connect with your audience. It takes the right skillset to make that connection develop into something beyond another meeting on your customer's calendar. This book provides you with that skill set. I'll refer to technology only in terms of what is needed to make it easy for your audience to see you, hear you, and relate to you, and how to use that technology to connect with your audience.

INTRODUCTION: AS GOOD AS IT GETS?

Take a bow if you rose to the challenge of connecting with your customers, partners, or teams when the 2020 pandemic hit. You deserve applause for having made a lot of big changes in a short window of time. But since this is a book about building relationships, I'm going to be honest with you. That initial bar was pretty low:

Got a Zoom account? Check.
Camera on? Check.
Find a spot where the family won't wander in half-naked? Umm... Check.

Initially, we were so delighted to have the ability to hear and see each other again that turning on our camera seemed sufficient. Then we quickly became immersed in the tools and technology, like platforms, backgrounds, microphones, polls, virtual whiteboards, nifty animations, and magnifications, to support our efforts to connect with customers. With each tool, we imagined getting ever closer to recreating that in-person experience. I think most would agree that this approach has fallen far short of expectations. Managing tools is not the same as managing relationships.

After perhaps dozens, hundreds, or even thousands of video calls or meetings you may feel like you have the mechanics to connect on video, but the experience feels quite... mechanical. In addition to the physical distance created by virtual communications, there is a gaping emotional divide that stretches between you and your customer, straining existing relationships and keeping new ones from getting past "you're on mute."

The sheer efficiency of video meetings and calls leaves a fraction of the time previously allotted for small talk vs. when in person. Being the third, fourth, or fifth video call in a buyer's afternoon makes it increasingly difficult to stand out. In a growing backlash against the demands of being on camera, more buyers are leaving their video off, severely limiting a seller's ability to pick up cues or gauge reactions. And, even if a buyer is on video, there is limited body language visible to read. Multiple people on a call simply compound the challenge of connecting individually and make reading the room a physical impossibility. Eye contact, a major component of relationship-building, is nearly non-existent on video calls and meetings—and even those who know better continue to stare at their screens.

Is Relationship Selling Possible on Video?

It's not your imagination. Relationship-selling has taken a big hit. Those face-to-face interactions with customers or team members, whether planned or spontaneous, provided valuable shared experiences and opportunities to read and share a full range of expressions and emotions. Video, as the business world is currently using it, has been mostly unable to offer a sufficient substitute for all of those relationship-building touches that used to take place with your buyer. The lunches, the coffees, the golf outings, or the simple hallway or pre-meeting conversations are all casualties of the pandemic and a blow for relationship sellers everywhere.

According to *Harvard Business Review*, building new relationships has proven especially difficult in a virtual world:

"With limited or no opportunity to meet in person, buyers naturally turn to known, trusted suppliers who already understand their business needs. For sellers, this makes access to prospective buyers the first chokepoint. And if sellers do get access, virtual-only connection makes it difficult to address additional challenges of winning new customers."[i]

This is bad news unless, of course, you're sitting on an endless supply of satisfied, risk-averse customers or loyal partners. But if your goal is to establish new relationships—the life and blood of sales—or shore up existing relationships to withstand competitive overtures and future obstacles, you can't afford to sit back and watch your pipeline dry up.

Working-from-home and the rapidly evolving business landscape has changed the world dramatically. It's my belief, and many others, that its impact will continue on a long horizon. Those initial meetings in particular, where relationships are the hardest to achieve, will likely be conducted by video as companies continue to take advantage of cost-savings. As companies find more ways to use video to communicate with customers, the virtual world becomes an increasingly competitive and demanding arena in which to differentiate, be heard, and connect with others in a meaningful way.

It's no wonder that Gartner's recent forecast predicting that eighty percent of B2B sales will take place virtually in 2025 is met with less than enthusiastic applause.[ii]

It's enough to make a salesperson exclaim, "Is this as good as it gets?" I assure you; it is not.

Envision...
a virtual meeting where both you and your customer feel as if you are sitting across from each other having a cup of coffee. Your eye contact makes your customer feel like they are really getting to know you. When they speak it makes them feel both heard and understood. Your face and body language add context and emotion to your words. You are able to read your customer's cues without constantly breaking eye contact with them, and you accurately interpret those cues and respond to them accordingly. Your customer is engaged and responsive, and your relationship progresses with each meeting. You are creating a near in-person experience for your customer, building a strong foundation for new relationships, and enhancing the foundation of established ones.

Is this vision even possible?

The answer is yes.

Most people have been trying to close this virtual gap with tools and technology. But the tools and technology only give you the potential to connect with buyers. They are the enabler, not the solution. Tools can't make that connection between you and your buyer meaningful or memorable. Tools can't build a relationship through the camera for you. For that, you need new skills. And that's what this book is about.

Hey, I Know You!

Perhaps you've experienced that feeling of knowing someone whom you've never met in person and only seen on a screen. Whether it's Jimmy Kimmel, Brene Brown, a Peloton instructor, or a local sportscaster, you may feel as if you could easily sit down and slip into a conversation with that person over a beer or a cup of coffee. Perhaps you've just assumed that actors, broadcasters, presenters, and influencers are born with a natural ability to connect effortlessly with a virtual audience. That couldn't be further from the truth. They had to learn a specific skill set to transcend the big or small screen and establish a personal relationship with each person on the other side of it. I know because I was one of those actors.

I enrolled in an acting class shortly after landing my first sales job. Surrounded by extroverts on my sales team, acting seemed like a quick way to boost my confidence, like firewalking but less painful. The short story is it worked. I learned more about quickly building relationships, collaborating with others, and delivering an impactful message as an actor than through any sales training program I'd taken.

After two years of selling by day and performing on stage by night, I was invited to audition for a small role in an independent film. I prepared the same way I did for a live theatrical audition. I studied my lines, analyzed my character, and warmed up physically and vocally.

Audition day arrived and I set out with the same confidence I felt going into a client meeting fully prepared. When I stood in front of the camera and the casting director bellowed, "action," my confidence disappeared. I suddenly realized that I didn't know where to direct my gaze. *Should I stare at the camera? Should I make eye contact with the other actor?* When I opened my mouth to speak, nothing came out.

The casting director asked me if I would like to start again. I nodded, located the line in my script, and forged ahead. I felt like I was speaking into a vacuum. My hands hung at my sides like dead weight. *Did I normally use them when I spoke?* If so, I certainly couldn't remember how. After an excruciating two minutes, the director yelled, "Cut."

Spoiler alert: I did not win that part. Later that day, I shared my audition nightmare with an actor friend.

> *"Did you take any on-camera classes?"*
> *She asked, cocking her head.*
> *I shook my head.*
> *"Why not?"*

I considered her question. I just assumed that my years of selling, presenting and performing face-to-face had prepared me to speak, stand, and behave like a normal human being in front of a camera. My friend laughed at my naivete and gave me the phone number for a good on-camera coach.

Every Tuesday for eight weeks I walked to a dank basement studio in New York City's West Village to learn from an Emmy-nominated director what it took to be authentic in an artificial environment—which is what being in front of a camera is. Almost immediately I began booking roles in television shows, national commercials, and films. I even landed a spot on an episode of the popular HBO series, *Sex and the City.*

Sorting Through the Noise

During the pandemic, I watched as the entire sales community struggled with the same challenges that I had encountered as an actor, without any of the solutions I had been fortunate enough to learn. I, like many of you, read countless confusing and often conflicting pieces of advice about how to communicate on video, most of it from people who had never worked in front of a camera, advice like:

- Look at the customer/Look at your screen/Look at the camera
- Be yourself/Be bigger/Be smaller
- Use your hands/Don't use your hands
- Use a virtual background/Don't use a virtual background
- Stand up/Sit down

It was bewildering, to say the least. So, I sprang into action. I created the Selling On Video Master Class, adapting professional on-camera techniques to the practicalities of communicating in a virtual business environment. To date, more than five-thousand people have taken this class and overcome many of the challenges mentioned above.

This book, like my Master Class, is drawn from my experience as an actor, a presentation expert and the thousands of business leaders, sellers, marketers, and professional speakers I have coached on applying these skills to real-life situations. It allows me to reach you, who like many, may be frustrated with the current state of their virtual relationships and strongly suspect that this is not as good as it gets. In these pages I share not just why you need to adapt, but specific methods and tactics for connecting on a deeper level with customers, partners, or teams to create that near in-person experience on live or recorded video. In the chapters ahead you'll learn how to:

- Build and strengthen relationships with eye contact, gestures, and active listening.
- Convey credibility, authenticity, and empathy through expression and intonation.

- Increase engagement and interaction with passive, virtual audiences.
- Read and more accurately interpret customer body language on video.
- Engage in dynamic two-way conversations—whether your audience is on video or not.
- Maintain engagement with your audience while managing slides, screens, scripts, participants, and tools.

How to Read This Book

This book delivers a full guide and instructions for connecting, differentiating, and building a more meaningful relationship with your audience on video. Each chapter focuses on a specific skill set. Not every technique will speak to you, and that's OK. But don't be too quick to throw an idea out if there's a possibility that it might help improve your connection with your audience.

Like learning any language, you'll have greater success if you start by learning the alphabet, which in this book are the five essential qualities necessary to build a relationship that are often missing in video communication in Chapter 1. In Chapter 2, you'll gain critical awareness into how the camera (and thus your customer) sees you and interprets your behavior.

In Chapter 3, you'll discover how actors and other on-camera professionals "cheat" for the camera to benefit their audience, and how you can apply these same techniques for your customer's benefit. Chapter 4 provides you with helpful advice for using your technology—the lights, cameras, mics, and more—to make it easy for your customer to connect with you. You'll also get tips from on-camera pros for how to look and sound your best with the right virtual setup, background, clothing, makeup, and hairstyles.

In Chapter 5, you'll learn how to look people in the eye on video and break through that virtual wall that currently exists between you and your audience. And in Chapters 6 and 7, you'll discover two ways to read body language without constantly breaking eye contact with your audience, as well as what the differences are between on-screen and in-person body language, and how to respond accordingly.

Chapters 8, 9, and 10 show you how to use your communication tools, your face, body, and voice, to add context and emotion to your video calls and meetings. In Chapters 11 and 12, you'll learn how to turn passive, virtual customers into active participants and how to maintain engagement with your audience while managing slides, scripts, notes, multiple screens or cameras.

Finally, you'll learn a proven program for practicing and evaluating your performance as painlessly as possible by adopting a director's perspective in Chapter 13.

Let's Get Started!

Reading this book is only the start. In order to break long-standing habits and behaviors that you've developed over the years, you also need to get these skills into your mind and body. That's why most chapters include simple exercises to help you practice at your own pace. Take your time. Master one skill at a time. Don't try to implement them all at once or you may soon be overwhelmed. It took you years to learn how to build relationships face-to-face. Give your virtual relationship-building skills more than a few days to take root!

Once you have built a solid foundation with these skills, your confidence will soar and your natural personality and energy will shine on video. Your relationships will be deeper and more meaningful and your audience more engaged and responsive.

Are you ready to look your audience in the eye? Cue Lights, Camera, and ACTION!

CHAPTER 1

THE MISSING BUILDING BLOCKS OF VIRTUAL RELATIONSHIPS

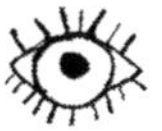

The greatest problem in communication is the illusion that it has been accomplished.

GEORGE BERNARD SHAW, PLAYWRIGHT

If you've ever been on a dreadful first date or had an office mate you did not click with, you know that relationships don't happen simply by putting two people together in a room. Like any living, breathing organism, relationships require certain elements to grow and flourish, regardless of whether you are communicating face-to-face or virtually.

The Missing Chemical in Virtual Relationships

One of those necessary elements is actually a chemical: Oxytocin, otherwise known as the love hormone. You may be wondering whether a love hormone is appropriate for a business relationship, but oxytocin is responsible for more than just feelings of attraction. It helps us to trust people and feel more connected.[iii] While oxytocin is activated easily in person, it's much more difficult to achieve on video, at least, the way people are currently using video.

The first way to activate oxytocin is through eye contact. Direct eye contact raises your level of oxytocin and reduces the level of cortisol, the hormone that creates stress.[iv] This combination makes us feel more connected, open, and relaxed with the person making eye contact. The second way oxytocin is released is through physical contact, like shaking hands. While we're unable to achieve that physical connection on video, there is strong evidence that just seeing someone's hands can put people at ease, build trust, and facilitate a connection.[v]

The 5 Missing Qualities on Video

Experts tend to agree that there are also five essential qualities which must be present for a relationship to develop: authenticity, an interest in others, being a good listener, empathy, and trustworthiness. While sellers may easily check those boxes when meeting with a customer in person, most fail to express these qualities on video adequately. Many sellers lack the awareness of how the camera reads and the customer interprets behavior on video, and the know-how to successfully adapt to these new realities. This results in misunderstandings, miscommunication, and missed opportunities for a relationship to take root. More recent relationships especially suffer as sellers haven't earned enough goodwill with prospects to merit the benefit of the doubt when sellers fall short on their efforts to connect.

In this chapter, you'll see how each of these building blocks to forming a solid relationship with your customer is impaired by video and how you can start the process of rebuilding.

1. AUTHENTICITY

The camera is a pretty accurate lie detector. And so are humans. If you try to be someone you are not on video, you will appear insincere, incongruent, or downright phony to your audience. No one sets out to be inauthentic on video; however, people often behave very differently on video than in person. It may be nerves and the constraints of the medium, or it may be the fact that the camera does not pick up certain nuances that present a much fuller picture of you to your customer when in person.

For example, certain behaviors or mannerisms that were considered charming or quirky when sharing the same space with your audience fail to translate effectively on video and make otherwise confident sellers appear nervous and uncertain. Many sellers who are quite charismatic in person appear wooden and devoid of personality on video because the camera waters down their natural energy and enthusiasm. Add to this the challenges of managing a new layer of technology, a camera, and a customer they can barely see (if at all), and it's a wonder any personality comes through!

Alternately, many people confuse authenticity on video with being natural or comfortable. This common mistake results in countless bland, low-energy interactions that are forgotten by a customer as soon as they sign off. Yet some salespeople cling to this pseudo-authenticity as an excuse to continue doing what they did face-to-face on video with an adamant: "I just want to be myself!" While this is a well-intentioned goal, it's helpful to remember that almost everything you learned to do was unnatural at first. Tying a shoelace, driving a car, or giving a speech were not skills bestowed upon you at birth. But you somehow found a way to internalize those behaviors and call upon them as needed. Are you being fake because these behaviors were acquired? If the answer is no, it's hard to argue against learning new skills to be successful in a new medium. And yet, many do.

To communicate more effectively on video and build meaningful relationships, there are certain behaviors we need to adapt, and some new ones we need to acquire. And we can accomplish all of this while still remaining authentic and true to ourselves. Many of the techniques you'll learn are used by actors on film and television. You may be thinking, what do actors know about being authentic?

Acting and Authenticity.

With any part you play, there is a certain amount of yourself in it. There has to be, otherwise, it's just not acting. It's lying.

JOHNNY DEPP, ACTOR

Responding authentically is a strong tenet of modern acting and modern selling. It's what makes you relatable. On screen, this relatability is valid whether an actor is playing a character in the contemporary world or a sci-fi fantasy. While Captain Jack Sparrow in *Pirates of the Caribbean* lives in an entirely fictional world, you relate to him because of the realistic way that he responds to often unnatural circumstances *(and maybe because of his wicked sense of humor as well).*

And like it or not, you, my virtual friend, are in some unnatural circumstances as well when you are on video. But, like a modern actor, you too can learn to adapt to your environment in a way that is realistic and relatable to your audience while remaining true to yourself.

2. **EXPRESSING INTEREST.**

Relationships thrive when each person is interested in how the other sees and experiences the world around them, not merely how that person can help them achieve their goal. With limited opportunities to engage in small talk on video, it's difficult to get a chance to ask questions outside of the meeting agenda, which may make you appear uninterested and self-serving on video.

In addition, in the mixed-up world of video where rules like left is right and if the camera didn't see it, it didn't happen, much of the body language and facial expressions sellers unconsciously exhibit on video comes across as inattentive to customers.

3. **BEING A GREAT LISTENER.**

Listening attentively is one of the biggest compliments you can pay someone. Unfortunately, listening gets a whole lot trickier on video. People are much more passive when they're in front of a screen, giving you a whole lot less to actually listen to! The larger the audience, the more pronounced the silence. When sellers rush to fill these uncomfortable gaps or answer their own questions, they further limit a customer's expression.

When customers do speak, sellers rarely exhibit any of the signs associated with listening used in person; those verbal acknowledgments, *uh-huh*, or *mmhmm*, are lost due to the limits of technology.

Even those small nonverbal signals, the head nod, the raised eyebrows, the encouraging smile, are often missing on video. Not to mention the complete lack of eye contact most customers receive when they do open their mouths to speak.

Have you ever been talking to someone at a party or networking event who was constantly scanning the room for someone more important to talk to? In that case, you know exactly how unsatisfying this experience feels. This is what your customer experiences when you fail to look them in the eye. And on video, the camera is the eyes of your customer.

The result?
Customers feel unheard and unseen even when they do share.

4. EXHIBITING EMPATHY.

Listening without showing compassion or understanding can make your buyer feel like a slide under a microscope. It's not enough to feel empathetic on video; you must be able to reflect back to your customer that you understand and care about what they're saying in more than words. Like listening, this quality is easily lost in virtual communications as sellers are either too distracted to react or unaware that their face, body, or tone is not communicating those feelings adequately on camera.

Some of the empathetic body language we use in person, like leaning forward or nodding, can take on a more aggressive meaning on video. Further complicating matters, customers often have their camera off, leaving sellers in the dark regarding what the customer is thinking or feeling. If they do have their cameras on, typical on-screen behavior masks many of those feelings that you'd be able to pick up on easily in person. As one salesperson observed after a painfully one-sided video meeting, "all I see is a whole bunch of blank faces staring at their screens." This begs the question, what exactly are you supposed to react to?

5. TRUSTWORTHINESS.

Establishing trust and credibility is the foundation of any relationship—both personal and business. While your credibility is likely no different in person than on video, your behavior in front of the camera can call that credibility into question. For example, research has found that we are more likely to trust a person who looks us directly in the eye.[vii] With the shortage of eye contact taking place on video, it's surprising that any business is getting done at all! You may think that some eye contact is better than none, but unfortunately, that is not the case. Quality and accuracy matter on video. People whose gaze jumps from camera to screen, screen to notes, then back to the camera may appear shifty-eyed and suspicious.

Another challenge to building trust on video is that most people don't show their hands. In a TEDx speech, body language expert Allan Pease shows how open palm gestures send trust signals to other people's brains, making them feel less threatened and more receptive.[viii] It makes sense if you think about it. Open hands indicate we aren't hiding anything behind our back (or off-camera) and can be trusted. The "talking head view" that most people adopt on video makes it difficult or awkward to include gestures. When people do gesture, their lack of clarity and readability on video contribute more to confusion than credibility.

Interestingly, people decide in the first few seconds of meeting you whether you're trustworthy.[ix] Much of this first impression is based on nonverbal signals. I mean, how much can you say in three seconds?! That's why it's critical to know what your body is communicating to your audience. Most people don't have any idea. They assume their intentions match their actions. Yet what I see on video is body language that is mostly incongruent with what the person is saying or trying to convey. Studies reveal that we don't trust people whose body language says one thing while their words say something else.[x] Yet how many times on video does someone say, "I'm happy to see you," or "I'm so sorry to hear that," with a blank expression on their face? In person, your body language and energy might balance things out. As you'll learn, on video, if it's not in the frame, it never happened. On the other hand, unconscious tics or nervous movements take on larger-than-life proportions on video, which can undermine your efforts to build relationships and trust.

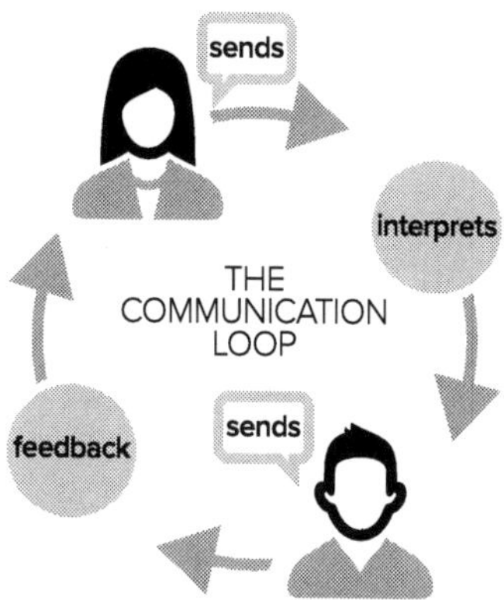

The Broken Virtual Communication Loop

We express any ideas, thoughts, or emotions, including these five essential qualities, through what's known as a communication loop.[xi] This simply means that the sender sends a message, the receiver interprets it, and then provides feedback to the sender, confirming their receipt. (See diagram.)

In person, the communication loop often takes place wordlessly and without interruption, as follows:

1. Seller smiles (sending the message that they are pleased to see the customer).
2. Customer interprets it correctly.
3. Customer smiles back (providing feedback that they received the message, interpreted it correctly, and sending a new message that they are happy to see the seller).

Based on the customer's response, the seller can now confidently engage in a conversation. And so, the cycle continues: sending, receiving, and providing feedback. Unfortunately, this natural process is often disrupted in a virtual world, breaking down at one or more of these three critical stages.

STAGE 1: MESSAGE BREAKDOWN

When the seller thinks they are sending one message, but they are actually sending a different message, this breakdown occurs. Whether the difference is because the message is distorted by the camera, not visible or audible to the customer, or requires greater context, is irrelevant. The damage is done. Here's an example of a message breakdown:

1. Seller thinks they are showing attentiveness because they are staring at the customer's image on the screen (and not their webcam).
2. Customer interprets that the Seller is distracted or uninterested in anything beyond a sale.
3. Customer becomes unresponsive and cuts the call short and the Seller is left confused and disappointed.

STAGE 2: INTERPRETATION BREAKDOWN

Certain behaviors, movements, gestures, and expressions mean different things on screen than they do face-to-face. Assigning in-person meaning to on-screen behavior often leads to confusion and miscommunication, as you'll see below:

1. Customer has a blank expression on their face as the Seller is speaking.
2. Seller incorrectly interprets this expression as boredom or impatience and races ahead in their presentation, trying to find something that sparks interest with their customer.
3. Customer (who was not initially bored or impatient) sees what appears to be a disorganized or rushed Seller and interprets this as a lack of credibility or interest on the Seller's part. The Customer's

expression remains blank (or shows signs of disinterest), further fueling the Seller's panic.

STAGE 3: FEEDBACK BREAKDOWN

Sending a message and receiving no feedback at all is much more common on video than in face-to-face interactions. Can you imagine if you were sitting across from a customer in-person and asked them a question, and they just sat silently, staring at their desk? You'd be right to feel concerned. The equivalent to this happens all the time on video and produces needless and detrimental stress and anxiety for sellers.

For example:

1. Seller asks a question to a small group of customers who are not on video.
2. Despite hearing the question, customers remain silent, either contemplating an answer or waiting for one of their peers to respond.
3. After a short pause, Seller nervously answers their own question reinforcing for the audience that their participation is not expected.

Sadly, these breakdowns happen over and over, dozens of times on the same video call or meeting, compounding their impact and making relationships difficult or impossible to take hold. What is to be done, short of checking in with your audience after every message to confirm proper receipt, or ending each sentence with a desperate plea of, "Does that make sense?"

Being aware of how and why these frequent communication loop breakdowns take place is critical for avoiding misunderstandings, missed connections, awkward pauses, and unhealthy spikes of adrenaline.

If your objective is to build relationships on video, you need to express authenticity, attentiveness, interest, empathy, and credibility clearly and absolutely. You must learn to recognize where the communication loop is breaking down and develop an awareness of the verbal and nonverbal messages you're sending to your audience. You must also understand how to interpret your customer's on-screen behavior so that you communicate with confidence regardless of whether you receive visual confirmation of your message being received.

The chapters ahead will show you exactly how to do all of this.

CHAPTER 2

WHAT THE CAMERA SEES

The camera really loves her!

EVERY PERSON REFERRING TO ANYONE BUT THEMSELVES

There's often a long break between shots when filming television shows on location as crews readjust the lights, cameras, and sound equipment for the next scene. During that time actors often congregate around the craft services table for snacks, networking, and a chance to run into one of the lead actors. It was on such a break during a shoot for HBO's *Sex and The City* that an attractive, reed-thin man with jet black hair stood across from me, filling his plate. As a day player (an actor with a limited role) I was tired and famished after a 12-plus-hour day, so I didn't pay him much attention.

When I returned to my table the other actors jumped on me before I could take my seat, "Oh my God! Did you talk to Kyle MacLachlan?"

My head jerked up. *Kyle MacLachlan? Was that guy in the super skinny jeans Kyle MacLachlan, aka, Charlotte's husband in Sex and the City, and Dale Cooper in Twin Peaks?* Spotting him again in the crowd, I instantly recognized him. After kicking myself for not starting up a conversation with Kyle mid-scoop, I was shocked at just how thin he was in person compared to on my television screen.

You've probably heard the saying—the camera adds ten pounds *(sorry, but it's true!).*[xii] But extra weight is just one of the tricks the camera can play on you and your audience. As the window to your customer's eyes, you can't afford to be in the dark about how the camera reads people, objects, movement, and color, for example.

Understanding what the camera sees and thus how your customer experiences you and your message on their screen is a vital first step to repairing that broken communication loop and creating a near in-person experience for your audience.

The Camera (and Your Customer) Sees You in 2D.

The reason for the extra ten pounds *(and the occasional double chin!)* is because the camera cannot read depth, making both objects and people appear flat on screen. While additional weight is few people's best friend, the bigger problem associated with this two-dimensional view is how lifeless and impassive most people appear on video. In person, our physical presence sends a myriad of signals to our audience. Without the full picture you present when face-to-face with a customer, your face must carry a lot more weight *(no pun intended)* on video to communicate that same level of energy, context, and emotion.

The Camera Provides a Reverse Image of You.

In my experience, few people see themselves on video and say, "You know what? I look fantastic!" One of the many reasons for this is that for however many years you've been on this planet, the vast majority of exposure to your own face has been through your reflection in a mirror. The camera picks up the reverse of that mirror image. Unless you have a perfectly symmetrical face *(which is unlikely, unless you're Jennifer Biel)* it's often quite a shock to see how others see you. And, if you're like most people, you are less than pleased with the results. In fact, I surveyed nearly one thousand salespeople about their biggest challenges concerning being on video and disliking how they looked or sounded made the top three (right after the inability to make eye contact or read body language).

PRO TIP

While there are certainly some physical and technical adjustments you can make that may improve the way you look and sound on camera (see Chapter 4), **I recommend hiding your image when you're on a video call. Besides being a magnet for your attention, seeing yourself on video places the focus on you, rather than where it belongs, on your audience.**

The Camera Reads Feelings.

Acting's all about the confidence you exude, especially on film. I mean, nervousness isn't attractive in anyone, but a film camera will seek it out and punish you.

JOHN C. REILLY, ACTOR

How can an inanimate object possibly know how you're feeling? The camera is objective, picking up what it sees, but also what you feel because your feelings are written all over your face. Whether you are aware of it or not, your feelings come out through your eyes, your facial expressions, the way you move and speak. There's no hiding from the camera or the human eye.

You've probably heard or even used the expression—the camera really loves her (or him.) For me, this was immediately followed by, *well, it may love her, but it sure as heck isn't crazy about me!* Perhaps you feel the same. But the truth is that the camera is objective. It simply records what it sees. People who shine on video are not loved by the camera, but rather they love, or at least like, the camera. And if you don't like the camera? Well, that's a problem.

The camera does not care what the source of your negative feelings is either. If you feel any apprehension, dislike, or discomfort, it will be communicated to your audience. For most people, this uneasiness is associated with the unnatural act of being on camera or communicating virtually. As one seller commented to me recently, "I am so over virtual meetings!" I empathize with the sentiment, but it's dangerous. You can't simply turn your feelings on or off the minute you turn your camera on. So while your words may say, "I'm happy to be here," your eyes, your face, or your demeanor will shout, "I can't wait to get off this call!" Since research shows humans instinctively distrust people whose words and body language are at odds with each other this incongruency can sow seeds of doubt in your audience.

While it may sound silly, this is why it's important to love your camera, or at least learn to like it.

Making Friends with Your Camera

The main relationship in the whole series was the one between the camera and Fleabag. I had to convince myself that whoever was watching on the other side of the camera was instantly complicit with Fleabag and instantly a friend of hers.

PHOEBE WALLER-BRIDGE, ACTOR

Your camera is the vehicle through which you communicate with your audience, therefore, you must think of it as a friendly entity, not a force working against you, judging every misstep or minor infraction. So how do you develop a friendly relationship with this inanimate object? Like any friendship, you have to work at it. If you've been in an adversarial relationship with your camera for a while, now is the time to start fresh. Spend a couple of minutes every day talking to your camera. Here's an example of how that conversation might go:

DAY ONE: "Hello, camera. I feel silly talking to you, but I was told that it would help me build stronger relationships with my customers. So here goes ..."

DAY TWO: "I'm back for more! Let's see, I guess I'll tell you about my day. I've got a meeting with a potential client this morning, and this afternoon I'm looking forward to catching up with the rest of my team."

DAY THREE: "Hey camera, I had the craziest call with this prospect yesterday...

The bottom line is this: Don't let how you feel about being on camera get in the way of communicating freely with your customer.

The Camera Picks Up (Most) Subtleties.

If you've ever been in a conversation with someone whose gaze is just slightly above, below, or to the side of your eyes, you know how distracting that is. While I appreciate the effort on video, just missing the mark with eye contact is almost as bad as no eye contact at all. Most people don't realize just how precisely the camera reads certain things, like the focal point of the eyes, the lift in the brow, or the tensing of the jaw.[xiii] While these subtle details may go unnoticed in person, they stand out in glorious high definition detail on camera, creating distractions or contributing to an undeserved poor impression.

Being aware of what your face and body are communicating to your audience is critical on video. The only way to build this awareness is by watching your recordings. I hear you groan. But don't worry. You'll learn a more constructive and less painful way to do that at the end of this book.

The Camera Reads Energy.

You need to up your energy level to make up for both sides of the conversation because the camera takes away that energy.

JEN MUELLER

SIDELINE REPORTER FOR THE SEATTLE SEAHAWKS

While the camera may add ten pounds, a lesser-known assumption is that it can take away ten to fifty percent of your energy. And sitting at home in your favorite chair isn't helping! So how do you bring enough energy and passion to your video calls to keep your customers engaged without blowing them away? And why does energy matter, anyway?

Sales is a transfer of energy. And nowhere is that energy weaker than when a salesperson is on video. There are a number of reasons for this. Your physical presence is missing; energy has to work harder to travel through the screen to your customer; salespeople are usually seated (when energy is at its lowest); and most people tend to flatten out their personality, delivery, and style when in front of a camera. Many times, this takes place because sellers confuse being natural with being comfortable.

Being Natural vs. Being Comfortable

I hear a lot of advice about being natural on video along with some interesting interpretations of what that means. For example, associating being natural with being comfortable results in frighteningly dull video calls or meetings. It's likely you've attended some of them. The quest to do only what feels comfortable or natural on video often leads to the following ineffective behavior:

1. **Low energy.** When you are comfortable, your energy is typically suppressed. This is fine if you're chilling on your couch or talking to your inner circle, but on camera low energy appears as disinterest, lethargy, or boredom to your audience. Since the camera naturally depletes some of your energy, putting comfort first simply exacerbates the problem. And, since most people engage on video while seated (a low energy position), it's doubly problematic.
2. **Inattentive posture.** When you're comfortable, your posture changes. You may lean back, slouch, or prop yourself up on your elbows. While certainly comfortable, these positions look to your audience like you're not fully committed to engaging in a conversation or establishing a connection.
3. **Passionless vocals.** Your voice, one of your primary tools for keeping your audience engaged, has less power, variety, and range when you're comfortable. With so many distractions within your customer's reach you can't afford to fall into a deadly monotone.
4. **Lifeless faces.** When relaxed and comfortable, your face is often a blank slate because you've released all tension—both good and bad.

I'm not suggesting you must be uncomfortable to be effective on video, but blindly pursuing comfort and throwing out behavior that feels initially uncomfortable or unnatural will hinder your efforts to connect with your audience beyond a surface level.

Finding the Right Energy for Video

How much energy do you need to bring to a video call, meeting, or recording? If I took a snapshot of you at different times throughout the day, I likely would see a wide range of different energies, depending on the situation. From you on the couch channel surfing, to you up on your feet rooting for your child's sports team, to you sitting down to a very appetizing meal—these all represent very different energy levels. The type of energy that reads well on video is closest to the meal scenario. It's a combination of passion, animation, and attentiveness that you might exhibit in one of the following types of situations:

- During a conversation with a peer about a topic that you're both passionate about
- On a second date with someone *(first dates produce too much chaotic energy!).*
- Delivering a toast at your best friend's wedding, surrounded by friends

These are the types of energetic states that you want to aim for on your video calls and recordings to help to offset the natural energy depletion that takes place on video. Notice that all of these situations are authentic versions of you, but you are in a heightened state. You are not uptight and too nervous to speak, but you are also not so comfortable that you could lie down and take a nap. In other words, you are using positive tension.

Positive tension is using just the energy necessary to activate the muscles required to communicate and keep you attentive and energized. You never want to get rid of tension entirely. After all, it takes a certain amount of tension to produce a smile, raise your eyebrows, or speak with conviction.

Negative tension is any unnecessary muscle tension or activity that interferes with the free flow of energy in your body. Holding your stomach in or clenching your jaw are examples of negative tension that can dilute the power of your communication. For example, many people hold tension in their necks. When that is the case, a fair amount of your attention and energy is used trying either to relieve that tension or attempting to ignore it. You may be so used to carrying pain or tension that you are not consciously aware of it. Either way, the physical or mental energy that you are expending on negative tension takes away your focus and robs energy from your primary goal, which is connecting with your audience and communicating as impactfully as possible. The tension-releasing exercise at the end of this chapter is an effective way to identify and get rid of unwanted tension so you can deliver your best.

Ramping Up Your Energy

The vast majority of non-performers are under the mistaken belief that they can turn on that peak level of energy just as their customer joins the meeting or they hit the record button. Those who work in front of the spotlight laugh at such naivete. They understand how unrealistic it is to expect your body to go from zero to one hundred in the blink of an eye. By waiting to turn on the energy until the second you need it, you spend the first few minutes on video warming up on your audience. And with today's dwindling attention spans, you don't have the luxury of taking your time to hit your stride.

Those first few moments in front of your audience are critical. Don't waste them working out the kinks in your delivery or finding your zone. Give yourself adequate time to ramp up to your optimal state of energy before your call or recording. Here are some ways to find your best on-video energy:

Go Over-the-Top.

People rarely speak with as much energy or personality on video as they use in their personal lives. This pre-performance warm-up exercise can help raise your energy enough to allow your natural passion and personality to truly shine through in your virtual presentations, pitches, or conversations.

To go over-the-top, start by channeling your favorite over-the-top actor. Think Nicholas Cage, a late-career Al Pacino, or the *Homeland* version of Claire Danes. These actors are known for making big *(some say, too big)* choices in their roles. Still, the bulging eyes, shouting lines, fingers in your face, perfectly demonstrate how to get your energy up and your personality out before a call. Here's how it works:

EXERCISE:
GO OVER-THE-TOP

- Deliver your presentation, pitch, or script with as much excitement and energy as you can muster. When you feel like you've reached your limit, push yourself even further. Go even bigger! *(Think melodrama.)*
- Try emphasizing random words, using different volumes, or changing your tone.
- Bring your body into it by gesturing with large movements *(don't worry about staying within the camera frame for this exercise).*
- Most importantly, have some fun with it!

I know what you're thinking. You'd blow a client right out of their chair with the energy you put into 're putting into this exercise! Maybe... For many people, this serves as just that, a great warm-up and a launching point for their call, presentation, or recording. Immediately following an over-the-top read, they can deliver the same content on a live call with greater personality and energy without pushing.

Others I've worked with are surprised to find that attempting to go over-the-top actually produces just the right energy they need to summon on video. Rather than coming across as "too much," they appear, nicely energized. We're able to see parts of their personality that were previously hidden, hear new notes in their voice, and connect with the real person behind the role. In this instance, going over the top is not just a warm-up, but a baseline to bring to each video call or meeting.

To know which type of energy level showcases you at your best on video, record a few minutes of your pitch or presentation—both before and after doing this exercise—and send to a few trustworthy peers for an objective opinion.

Tap into Why It Matters.

Energy is the direct result of how much you care about what is happening.

TONY BARR

PRODUCER AND AUTHOR OF *ACTING FOR THE CAMERA*

If you are not interested in what you are talking about (or who you are talking to), or if there is little at stake on the call, it's unlikely you will feel very energized. In this case, you have to do the more difficult job of manufacturing your own energy. A much more direct route is to take the time to think about why you're talking to each specific person. What problem are you helping your customer or audience solve? What are the consequences if they don't solve the problem?

Raising the Stakes to Reveal Urgency

If you're in sales, you know the power of helping your customer to not just see but feel the urgency of solving their problem. What you may not realize is that it's equally important for you to feel that urgency as well.

To communicate energy and emotions conducive to building relationships, like empathy, interest, or excitement, you need to feel as passionate as possible about your customer's situation. Emotions don't respond to vague facts and intellectual ideas, so you may need to dig a little deeper into what specifically is at stake for your customer. In other words, why does it matter if they solve this problem, solve it now, or solve it with you?

A quick and effective way to understand the urgency of someone's situation is called raising the stakes. You've likely seen this used in films and television shows as a device to get you invested in the hero's journey. For example, if the hero doesn't find the bomb by midnight, the city will be destroyed. If the city is destroyed, the country will go to war. If the country goes to war... You've seen this movie, right? The stakes keep ratcheting until the hero has no choice but to employ every trick known to find that bomb. In the meantime, the audience is on the edge of their seats.

You may apply the same idea to your customer or team by asking them, or yourself: What is at stake? What are the consequences of no action, delayed action, or wrong action? As you uncover a consequence, continue to dig deeper by asking, and then what happens? Often you (and your customer) will realize that a decision that may have appeared inconsequential at first glance, has much greater consequences when played out.

Of course, you never want to manufacture fake urgency, but understanding what's at stake for your customer may spark your emotions and bring greater energy to your calls and meetings.

EXERCISE

RELEASE NEGATIVE TENSION.

The Tension Release Exercise was developed by director Lee Strasberg who influenced generations of actors, like Marlon Brando and James Dean, at the famed Actor's Studio in New York.[xiv] Strasberg called tension, "The occupational disease of the actor." Its effect can be just as damaging to those of us in the business spotlight.

Try this exercise before you get on a video call or meeting:

1. Sit in a straight-backed chair.
2. Starting with your head, tighten all the muscles in your face, your scalp, and your jaw.
3. Hold onto that tension for ten seconds, then release.
4. Continue to work your way down your body through individual muscle groups, tensing and releasing, paying special attention to areas which feel tight.

I recommend getting on your feet after this exercise to get your positive energy flowing. Try shaking your arms, your wrists, your legs, and your feet. Dance. Do the hokey pokey. Whatever you do, be sure to move loosely and fluidly, and engage your whole body.

CHAPTER 3

CHEATING FOR THE CAMERA

You don't want to be the guy whose back is to the camera in the emotional part of the movie. So, you have to be aware of the camera movement and what the camera's doing.

RUSSELL CROWE, ACTOR

This book is all about being the best version of yourself possible on video. To achieve this goal, you need to adapt to the realities and constraints of the camera so that your customer may experience you at your best. In other words, there are times when you will be called upon to cheat for the camera.

Cheating for the camera is a common technical direction given to actors on a film or video shoot. It often requires actors to position their face or body toward the camera, even if it feels a bit awkward or unnatural to do so, to make themselves more accessible to the audience. This is because the camera represents what the audience will see on the screen, which is different than what they would see in person.

For example, when two actors are talking to each other in a movie or on a television show, they often stand much closer together than they ever would in real life. *(These are sometimes called mouthwash scenes, as in "I sure hope the other actor used mouthwash!")* This unnatural closeness allows the audience to see both of their faces at the same time.

If the director wants to get a close-up of one actor speaking, they would remove the other actor and have the speaking actor say their lines directly to the camera so that we, the audience, experience what the actor is thinking or feeling.

BEHIND THE CAMERA

Next time you see a character on television who is typing on their computer, notice how they type with their head up. Most of us type with our heads and eyes down in real life, but that wouldn't allow the audience to see what the character is thinking as they're typing. So, the actor has to cheat "up" to maintain a higher sightline for the audience's benefit. ***(I had to do this in a commercial and my output on the computer was complete gibberish!)***

If you've presented face-to-face before, you've probably cheated for your customer's benefit as well. You may have positioned yourself in the front of the room to allow your audience to see and hear you as clearly as possible. You may have stood at a somewhat uncomfortable angle next to the screen, allowing your audience to see your slides as well as your face. You may have spoken louder or softer, depending on the room's acoustics or the size of the group. You may have toned down your level of animation for certain audiences and ramped it up for others. And if you've received presentation training, you may have learned to gesture away from your torso *(no Tyrannosaurus Rex arms!)*, walk a stage, or hold a pause longer than was comfortable to allow the audience to settle down or absorb what you've said.

In the same way, you must modify some of your behaviors on video for your audience's benefit. Will it feel natural at first? No. Just as typing on a keyboard did not feel natural the first few times. But that doesn't mean that it's inauthentic. It simply means that you have not internalized the behaviors yet. Given time and practice, these adjustments will start to feel natural.

Following are a few necessary on-camera cheats that will allow you to communicate your true intention on video more clearly to the benefit of your audience.

The Camera-Ready Position

In the small space of the camera frame, your posture plays an outsized role in creating a first impression. Slouching back in your chair says one thing while hovering with your face two inches from the camera says something entirely different. What would you like to communicate to your audience? If you're interested in establishing a relationship, you want to appear energized, attentive, and open immediately. The best way to do this is to assume a camera-ready position. Here's the best way to find it:

Begin by sitting upright, spine and neck lined up, feet planted on the floor. Now, keeping your back straight and your head in line, hinge forward from the hips 10 to 15 percent, as if you're on the edge of your seat and you can't wait to hear what the other person has to say. This is your new camera-ready position.

Are you comfortable? Likely the answer is no. Why? Because you don't regularly sit that way! And like any new activity or position, it's going to feel awkward at first, but I promise you will feel at ease and more attentive over time. One thing that you can do to make this more comfortable and remind you to lean forward slightly is to put a pillow behind your lower back.

Like any new behavior, you need to practice this position. Start by trying to maintain your camera-ready position on video calls with friends or family. That way when you get on a call where the stakes are higher, it won't feel so foreign.

If the Camera Doesn't See It, It Doesn't Exist.

Early in my acting career, I was rehearsing a scene that called for me to be head over heels in love with my partner *(whom I had met all of ten minutes earlier.)* When the director yelled, "Action!" I summoned up all of the inner joy that I could muster and recited my lines.

The director stopped me after a few sentences. "You don't seem that happy." I bristled. "But I am happy!" After all, I felt happy.

The more experienced actors on set averted their eyes. I had broken a cardinal rule of rehearsal: Never argue with the director. But I forged on, confident that the truth was on my side. The director listened patiently to me before suggesting that I try the scene again while he recorded it.

Anxious to be proven right, I repeated the scene. Afterward, the director beckoned me over to the camera. As we watched the take in silence, my stomach sank. Ugh. *He* was right. I did not look happy.

After a long moment, the director spoke. "It doesn't matter what you feel like you're doing. If the camera doesn't see it, it doesn't exist."

This lesson holds true whether you are a performer, a salesperson, a speaker, or the CEO of a company. **What you think, feel, or intend to communicate is irrelevant. If the camera (and your audience) doesn't see it, it doesn't exist.** If you remember from the communication loop, the true measure of successful communication is not that you sent the message, but that the audience clearly and accurately received your message. The consequences of inaccurately communicating a message on video may cost you a relationship, a deal, or even a job.

Throughout this book you're going to be introduced to many techniques to ensure your audience accurately receives your message on video. Two of the most important techniques are gesturing in frame and looking at the camera.

Gesture in Frame.

Pics or it didn't happen, as they say on Instagram. Your audience only sees (and believes) what happens within the boundaries of your screen. Therefore, you must become familiar with your frame, (i.e., the edges of your screen) so that you can manage what the customer sees and what they do not.

Gesturing is an important communication tool, and when used correctly, it can add emphasis, emotion, and meaning to your message. You may have noticed, however, that most gestures on video calls and recordings tend to skate across the bottom of your screen like a barely visible footer or they extend outside of the frame entirely.

For gestures to support your message on video instead of detract from it, you must learn to move effectively within the boundaries of your frame using muscle memory. Checking your own image to see if you're in or out of frame on a call only adds lack of eye contact to the list of things distancing you from your audience.

For most people, gesturing within frame requires raising the elbows and gesturing from a slightly elevated, but more visible, position. I recommend refraining from extending your arms outside of the frame too often as it reinforces the virtual distance between you and your audience. You'll learn more about gesturing, what works on video, what doesn't, and how to develop that muscle memory in Chapter 8.

Look at the Camera.

If you're not looking at the camera, you're not connecting with your audience.

JULIE HANSEN

Looking at the camera on a video call or meeting is perhaps the most complex and most crucial cheat of all. But the fact is, to foster a relationship and develop a connection with your customer, you must look at the camera.[xv] To make your customer feel seen and heard, you must look at the camera just as if you were looking into your customer's eyes. Not their nose, their chin, or their shoes. Their eyes. And the webcam is their eyes!

Yes, you can (and should) move your customer's image around on your screen so that it is as close to your camera lens as possible, but it's unlikely that it will be a perfect match—and if you have more than one person on the call, making direct eye contact becomes increasingly more complex. Learning how to look at the camera and carry on a conversation, pitch, or presentation with as much focus, passion, and intention as if that person was seated right in front of you is an incredibly powerful and necessary virtual cheat.

I know, I know. You're looking at your customer's image on your screen. But know this: while it feels like you're making eye contact, it doesn't read as eye contact to the other person. And your excuse doesn't change their experience. Unfortunately, having this knowledge alone is not enough to keep most people from looking at their screen, their office, or anywhere else other than the camera. If it were, there wouldn't be so much bad eye contact on video calls!

But take heart. Actors have been perfecting this skill for years, and you will learn how to as well in Chapter 5.

How Often Should You Look at the Camera?

In order to build a relationship with someone in person, research recommends you maintain eye contact about two-thirds of the time when face-to-face.[xvi] Many people struggle with maintaining that much eye contact when in person, and on video it's even worse. This is a real problem because I believe you should maintain eye contact with your audience 80 percent of the time or more on video.

Why more eye contact on video than in person? Because in person you share a common environment with your customer. When sitting across from them and you break eye contact to glance at your notes, observe a photo next to them, or take in their movements, your customer knows what you're looking at. They can see that you are still engaged. Not so on video. When you look away from your customer on video, they have no idea what you're looking at. *(If the camera doesn't see it, it doesn't exist.)* Are you checking your phone, your email, or reading from a script? Even if your customer gives you the benefit of the doubt and assumes you're looking at their image on your screen, they are likely to still feel as if you're inattentive or distracted. Those are the types of doubts that erode relationships.

There's no hiding on video either. With only your face and eyes to focus on, any movement you make with your eyes is obvious to even the most casual observer. Those occasional moments of privacy you had in person when you knew your customer wasn't looking at you don't exist on video. You, and your eyes, are always on stage.

So regardless of whether you look away from the camera to check your listener's body language, view your notes, or daydream out the window, if you're not looking at the camera you're not connecting with your customer.

If you're concerned about making too much eye contact, don't worry. No one is staring at your face on their screen 100 percent of the time. Your audience has complete control over the amount of eye contact they're comfortable maintaining with you. But by keeping your eyes on the camera, you make yourself available to connect with your audience when they do look at you. If they look at their screen and see your gaze is focused elsewhere, you have broken the connection with your audience and given them another excuse to disengage.

In the coming chapters, you will learn how to make all the necessary adjustments and cheats on video that benefit your audience and further your relationship as effortlessly as you currently do in person.

TEST:
HOW EFFECTIVE IS YOUR EYE CONTACT?

Do you know how well you're connecting with your audience? I've developed the following test to assess one measurement of a strong virtual connection, your current level of direct eye contact. This measurement will become your baseline, and when you take this test again at the end of the book, my goal is for you to see an increase of 25% or more in the amount of eye contact you're making with your virtual audience.

For this test you'll need a stopwatch and a recent recording of yourself on a medium to high-stakes video call, e.g., with a customer, a partner, or a larger audience. Stopwatch in hand, review your video following these steps:

1. Start the stopwatch every time your eyes in the recording meet your eyes as a viewer. Pause the timer whenever the "recorded you" breaks eye contact. Continue, starting and pausing as you go until the end of the call.
2. Take the total amount of time on your stopwatch and divide it by the total length of the call or meeting. Write down this percentage.
3. Find your percentage in one of the following ranges to see how you're doing.

TEST RESULTS

80% OR HIGHER: Congrats! You're in a very elite group! Imagine what you can do when you learn how to use that eye contact and your other virtual tools to deepen and further that connection with your audience!

67-79%: You're on your way, but don't stop here! While this may be a sufficient level of eye contact for building relationships in person, you need to up your game if you want to develop relationships on video. In this book you'll learn how to level up your eye contact by removing any blocks holding you back and discovering those critical moments where eye contact can make or break a relationship.

50-66%: Warning: Your eye contact is below the acceptable level for in-person relationships, which means your virtual relationships are at risk. As you learn how to apply greater eye contact you'll experience less audience tune out and a higher level of engagement. Won't that be nice?!

0-49%: Danger Will Robinson! Your audience doesn't know if you can see them or hear them. They're prey to distractions and competitive overtures. But take a deep breath. This is where most people start and you are in the right place. You will learn all you need to know about making direct, personal eye contact in these pages. So hang on, because dramatic improvements in your personal interactions on video are right around the corner.

CHAPTER 4

SETTING THE STAGE FOR A NEAR IN-PERSON EXPERIENCE

I've always considered myself to be just average talent and what I have is a ridiculous insane obsessiveness for practice and preparation.

WILL SMITH, ACTOR

You probably did not become a salesperson to talk to a camera or become an expert on lighting, greenscreens, and microphones. Yet here you are: the actor, the director, the set designer, and the camera crew. And, oh, yes, you need to meet your quota, motivate your team, or run your business, too! While this is not a book about virtual technology, I am going to share some insider tips on how to use that technology to create as near an in-person experience as possible for your audience.

Your Camera

You don't need a super expensive camera to build a relationship with someone on video, but there are some minimum acceptable standards that you must meet. The current standard is HD 1080p.[xvii] Fall below that, and your image will be grainy or fuzzy, making it more difficult for your customer to see your eyes, and thus, more difficult to connect with you.

Unfortunately, many laptops are equipped with a 720p camera, sacrificing quality in order to save space and meet the demands for ever-thinner computers. Some laptops have the camera positioned in such an awkward place that it makes one wonder if the designer ever operated a camera! Suppose your laptop does have a low-quality camera (non-HD or 720p or less) or its location requires an advanced yoga move to access. In that case, you'll need to invest in a webcam, a digital camera that attaches to your computer or sits on a stand.

Webcam Tips

At the time of writing this book, many high-quality 1080p webcams are available. As technology changes more quickly than this book can keep up, I won't try to list them all for you; however, you can check the latest recommendations or read some of the many reviews on the web. If you do use a webcam, I recommend investing in a solid tripod to give you more flexibility in finding the optimum position for your camera.

The next step up from 1080p is 4K resolution, or Ultra HD. 4K delivers four times the pixels and, therefore, four times the detail of 1080p. While this sounds fantastic, keep in mind that 4K eats up more bandwidth and you will also need a 4K monitor to truly appreciate the quality difference, as will your audience. Also, 4K is currently a big leap in price from 1080p.

Using Your Camera for Video Calls or Meetings

While the camera quality on phones is often better than many laptops, video meetings and recordings that take place on phones almost always lack professionalism and introduce distractions. It's obvious when a person is using the camera on their phone to join a meeting because:

1. You often have a better view of their ceiling than their face. This is because most people default to portrait mode when using their smartphone. While fine for phone calls, checking emails, and surfing the web, portrait mode cuts off your body unnaturally at the sides, limiting your ability to use gestures and doing little to foster that in-person experience.
2. It looks as if the seller is in an active earthquake zone. Video is very sensitive to movement. Those tiny quivers in your hands

while holding a phone may be unnoticeable to you, but create a series of distracting aftershocks for your audience.

PRO TIP:

If you do choose to use your phone, set it to landscape mode, and invest in a phone stand or tripod. A stand will help you shoot from a more consistent and favorable angle and limit unnecessary movement.

Using Your iPad or Tablet for Video Calls or Meetings

Tablets and iPads present challenges of their own on video. A dead giveaway that someone is using their iPad is the slightly off-center gaze of the user. There's a perfectly good reason for this: The camera on an iPad is located slightly off-center when used in landscape mode (which is how most people use their tablet). If you didn't know this, don't feel badly. I've seen many tech-savvy people stare at the center of the iPad quite certain they are making direct eye contact with me. Unfortunately, close scores you points in horseshoes, but not in eye contact. Looking slightly away from your customer's eyes does little to advance your relationship and calls into question where your focus and attention are directed.

PRO TIP:

Take the time to precisely locate where the camera is on your tablet (use a sticky note until you memorize the camera's exact location), and practice until you can find that spot with your eyes on demand.

Status and Camera Position

Your camera should be positioned at your eye level. Anything else is awkward, unflattering, or defeats your efforts to create a near in-person experience. Another important thing about camera position that is often overlooked is the role it plays in communicating status.

Status is an unspoken factor in any relationship.[xviii] We are constantly sizing up how we stand in relation to others. When you are looking down at your customer because your camera is too low, it subconsciously conveys superiority. When you are looking up at your customer because the camera is too high, it conveys inferiority that you may not feel *(not to mention spectacularly bad views of you, like up the nose, a double chin, top of the head, etc.)*. Ensuring that your camera is at eye level creates a more equal status between you and your audience.

Most people are poor judges of how they come across on video including what eye-level actually looks like. Otherwise, why would we see so many unflattering angles and views? Because of this, I encourage you to get a second opinion. Take a screenshot of yourself at what you consider to be eye level. Review the screenshot on your monitor and send it to a peer. You—and they—should be able to see your face straight on, without any tilt of your chin or forehead. Are you indeed eye level with your camera? Or does it look as if you are looking up or down at your viewer?

To achieve this sweet spot, you may need to adjust your head, laptop, chair, or camera up or down accordingly. Once at eye level, you may experiment with slightly different angles.

PRO TIP:

Some people find that raising the camera a fraction above their sightline and then angling it down ever so slightly produces a more flattering view for their audience (and may reduce the appearance of a double chin as well!)

The Perfect Distance from the Camera

You wouldn't sit six inches away from your customer in a face-to-face meeting, nor would you sit ten feet away. Yet you've likely seen the equivalent of both of these extremes on video calls. In person or on video, you want the perceived distance to be close enough to connect, without crossing into your customer's intimate space. Scientists say that the ideal personal distance between good friends or family is one-and-a-half to two-and-a-half feet. Keep in mind that the perception of "appropriate" personal space varies by cultures. People from the Middle East, Southern Europe, or South America stand closer together while those from some Northern European and Asian countries tend to stand farther apart.[xx]

Overstep those social and cultural boundaries and you risk making people uncomfortable. Under step and you make it difficult for your customer to see you and thus connect with you. Since most people you will be talking to are seated about 12-18 inches from their screen, sitting the same distance (adjusting for any cultural preferences) from your screen should put you at the optimal distance for relationship building to take place.

For most video calls, meetings, and recordings, you should position yourself in the center of the frame with an equal amount of space on each side of you. Again, think about where you would sit across from someone in person. It's unlikely you would sit anywhere but right across from them for ease of conversation. The exception is when your space constrains you, or you have a product, whiteboard, or content that you need to include in the frame.

The Medium Close-up

How much of your torso should your audience see on their screen? I get asked this all the time! Once you've determined the ideal distance from the camera and have it positioned at eye level, this should place you at either high chest or shoulder level. In film, this is referred to as a "medium close-up." A medium close-up is ideal for most business video calls and recordings because it directs the viewer's focus to your face and eyes while allowing for your customer to see some gestures and movement. *(And remember, being able to see your hands can help build trust.)*

In a medium close-up, you should be able to place a fist above your head and just about hit the edge of the frame. Any more than that and you are too low, any less than that, and you are moving into extreme close-up or "floating-head" territory. Extreme close-ups are used sparingly in film, and even then, primarily for quick reaction shots. They should be avoided entirely in business as they may appear too intimate or aggressive.

One Screen, Two Screens, Three Screens?

While you don't need multiple screens to carry on a simple video conversation, it is often handy to have a second screen when you are sharing or collaborating on content—like slides, documents, or software. It's easy to feel overwhelmed however, when you add an additional screen to the already challenging tasks of presenting, accessing notes, managing collaboration tools, and trying to engage with your audience. There is no one-size-fits-all answer here, but I can offer the following guidance:

Make the screen that contains your camera your primary screen. In other words, wherever you will be spending most of your time, make sure your camera is there. Like me, you've probably been on enough calls where you've seen nothing but the side of the presenter's face. Having your camera on your most-used screen will make it easier for you to maintain a visual connection with your audience, even as you access notes or navigate slides. Place the participant's panel just under your camera on your primary screen. That will put you in the best position to read body language and maintain eye contact–which you'll learn in Chapter 6.

Practice switching between screens and sharing content. It's awkward for everyone when you aren't sharing what you think you're sharing, or you "lose" something in the black hole between two screens. Set up some practice meetings with peers until you have made—and corrected—every mistake possible.

When you add multiple screens and cameras, you start to have more in common with a television director than the average Zoom user and may find the following technique helpful.

Think Like a Television Director: The Multiple Camera Technique

If you want to maximize eye contact with your audience and share content, it may be time to invest in a second camera. Even shows which are shot in front of a live TV audience use three or four cameras at once. This allows the director to get multiple views for the much larger audience watching at home. By using multiple cameras, the home audience can have an equivalent experience to that of the in-person audience.

Fortunately, you don't need three or four cameras to recreate this experience in your home office. All you need are two cameras: one in your laptop and an external webcam which you would place on your second screen. Now, whatever screen you are focused on, you can select the corresponding camera for that shot! Alternating cameras is easier to do in some platforms (like Zoom) than in others. Note that since the view your audience will see of you will be slightly different with each camera angle, you don't want to switch cameras back and forth at an alarming rate. This technique is most appropriate when you expect to spend an extended period of time (i.e., five minutes or more) on one screen before switching to the other.

PRO TIP:

Ensure both your cameras are the same resolution (1080p) to avoid a huge gap in quality and consider using a neutral virtual background to maintain consistency.

Sound

There is a reason you see a long list of credits for members of the sound crew at the end of a film. Sound quality and clarity are vital to the film's success as most audiences don't want to struggle to understand what is being said *(although certain actors, like Casey Affleck, certainly test the limits of this!).* The same is true of your customer. Poor sound quality gives a customer an easy excuse to tune out, so don't skimp. Your voice should sound crisp, clear, and close—as if you are face-to-face having a conversation in a quiet setting. You don't need to sound like a studio DJ *(in fact, that can work against you)*, but you also don't want to introduce unnecessary distractions.

Sound quality in film is subject to many variables, including microphone quality and placement, vocal power and enunciation, location acoustics, and much more. You have similar variables as well but lack the professional crew to assist you. Below are some insider tips that will help you dial in the optimal sound for your video calls, meetings, and recordings.

Microphones

The sound quality from most webcams and laptop microphones is usually insufficient to create that face-to-face experience you want. Unsure if your sound is adequate? Record yourself on your current microphone speaking at your normal volume and pace. Play it back on a high-quality speaker or a good headset. Does your voice sound far away? Is there any fuzziness to it? Do you sound as if you're speaking from inside a tin can? If the answer to any of these questions is yes, you need to invest in an external microphone.

There are even more choices for microphones than webcams, so you'll certainly have your pick. USB condenser microphones are a good choice as they are fairly sensitive and also easy to plug and play on your computer.

Mics take in sound from different angles. If you're working from home or in a shared environment, look for one with a cardioid polar pattern. That simply means it accepts sound primarily from the front, as opposed to the sides and the rear, potentially reducing the amount of background noise you introduce into your call.

If you do use an external microphone, avoid making your audience feel like they're a guest on your podcast *(unless you are hosting a podcast!)* by placing it just outside of your frame if possible. You may also find a mic stand or extending boom arm helpful to position your mic in the optimal spot.

How to Talk on a Microphone

Just place your mic in front of your mouth and speak, right? Sometimes, but sound is tricky, and each microphone and acoustic environment is different. Not speaking correctly into a mic can result in muddled, sharp, or otherwise unpleasant and distracting speech. Many factors influence how you sound on a mic, including how far the mic is from your mouth and the level and the angle at which it is set.

Your proximity to the mic will obviously determine the sound volume; however, it also affects the quality. The closer you are to the mic, the fuller (and louder) the sound will be. The farther away you are, the more distant you will sound, and the more reverb your audience will hear. But move too close and you run into new problems: your S's may sizzle, and your hard sounds such as P's, D's, and K's may pop. *(Note: If this is a recurring problem for you, you may want to invest in a pop-filter.)*[xxi] Your audience may even hear you swallow or breathe, which can be uncomfortably intimate.

A good rule of thumb is to place the mic four finger-widths away from your mouth. Some mics are more sensitive than others, so you'll need to play with the settings and distance and mark the spot which delivers the best sound.

Headsets

If you work in a shared or noisy environment, using a headset on your video calls may be the only way to have a focused conversation with your customer. But keep in mind that headsets work against fostering that in-person experience. For most calls and meetings, I strongly advise avoiding anything but the most low-profile in-ear versions. Too many headsets say, "You're cleared for landing!" as opposed to,

"I hear you."

If you are recording a video to send to a prospect, it's best to avoid headsets altogether as they can give off a strong call-center vibe. Instead, opt for either a stand-alone microphone or a wireless lavalier mic that clips onto your shirt or jacket and allows for flexibility in movement.

Make sure the mic on your headset is pointing straight at your mouth for the best quality. While the distance from mic to mouth may seem pre-determined on headsets, you will likely need to adjust it to find the exact distance that works for you. If your mic is too close to your nose, your audience will hear the unpleasant sound of you breathing in through your nostrils. If the sound is too sharp, try angling your mic slightly to the side of your mouth.

The Purpose of Your Background

I worked as an extra on several films and television shows where we were referred to affectionately as "background." The purpose of background is to create a tone, mood, or atmosphere to support the scene and the performers, not steal the show. On a video call, the background is there to support you as well. You are already competing for the sale and your customer's attention. Don't add competing with your own background to the mix.

Your background projects an image, professional or otherwise, to your customer. The hallmark of a good background is that it is neat, clutter-free, well-lit, and perhaps adds a spark of personality.

Location, Location, Location!

Without the confines of a traditional office setting, your location is often up to you. That may mean holding video calls or making recordings anywhere from your kitchen table to the captain's seat on the Starship Enterprise. But choose wisely. Unless your real environment provides a negative experience for your audience, I recommend using a real background whenever relationship matters.

The Leveling Power of Backgrounds

For decades, most B2B meetings have been held in one person's business location, (aside from the occasional restaurant, bar, or golf course). Video provides a unique opportunity to level the playing field and eliminate that unequal footing of being on someone else's turf.

Video meetings or calls may reveal quite a lot about you to your customer and your customer to you. Salespeople who may have complained in the past about customers not seeing them as a "real" person, now have the opportunity to welcome clients into their home, making sales calls more personal than ever before. This can be a great advantage as it humanizes you and allows clients to see you as more than just the face of your company. Personal elements, like books, pictures, or furnishings, may stimulate conversation and deepen connections.

One place where this leveling power can backfire was brought to my attention by a senior sales executive at a mid-size technology company. Her company sent out a survey after a company-wide Zoom meeting which revealed a surprising insight. Many employees working from makeshift offices at home shared that they felt demoralized upon seeing the executives' beautifully decorated, dedicated home offices. In this case, a glaring divide was reinforced, rather than erased.

Consider the status of your audience when choosing a background. Just like clothing, it's fine to be one step ahead of your audience, but when you leapfrog them by several levels, you establish barriers to building a relationship that can easily be avoided. In the case of this technology company, the executives would have been better off joining the meeting from a more humble spot or using a virtual background to avoid negative comparisons.

When to Use a Virtual Background

Sometimes your space is not ready for prime time viewing. Perhaps there is too much clutter, you're in the middle of a home repair project, or the only suitable space gives your customer more personal information than they need. *(Bedroom Zoomers, I'm talking to you!)* Then it's time to consider using a virtual background or green screen.

Considerations When Using a Virtual Background

Keep in mind that a virtual background adds another layer of artificiality to your relationship, so choose one that is understated and doesn't advertise that it's a virtual background. Save the funny and fantastical backgrounds for your friends and family. Humor and cultural references are very subjective, and you introduce the risk of offending your customer or highlighting your differences. Additionally, a background that features a giant cartoon character or a tiger ready to pounce can present an ongoing distraction that draws your audience away from the conversation.

You may have also noticed that body parts have a curious habit of disappearing and reappearing with movement on virtual backgrounds. Besides being distracting *(it's hard to focus when half of the speaker's face disappears)*, it reinforces the fact that you are talking through the wonders of technology. Many people don't realize that your natural background still needs to be neat and relatively clutter-free when using a virtual background. Here are a few more tricks for making this disappearing act less pronounced:

- **Slow down your movements.** The camera doesn't read fast movements well and virtual backgrounds only add to the distortion your audience sees.
- **Position yourself in front of a solid-colored wall.**
- **Make sure there's enough contrast between your hair, your clothing, and your background.**
- **Eliminate or limit any light coming from behind your background.**

- **Download the latest platform updates or drivers for your webcam.**

If you have a choice, take advantage of the benefits of a natural background whenever you can.

Lighting

No amount of makeup can make up for bad lighting.

HEARD ON FILM SETS

In film and television, lighting can create a tone or mood as well as impact how the audience perceives a particular actor. If the character is poorly lit, or in the shadows, we know they are probably up to no good. The same is true for video. We perceive someone differently if they're well lit, vs. lit like they're in a hostage video or a 1940's film noir. Being over lit is as ineffective as being under lit. Proper lighting allows your customer to see you as clearly and easily as if you were sitting across from them in person. It also highlights two of your most important communication tools: your facial expressions and your eyes.

Natural Lighting

You probably know by now that you always want to sit or stand facing your light source and that natural light is the best for video. That's because natural light disperses light more evenly than artificial lighting.

The problem with natural light is that it's not 100 percent reliable. The quality and intensity of the light are subject to change throughout the day. For example, at 9 a.m. every morning, the sun streams into my home office from two large windows, giving my face an other-worldly quality. For one of my clients, a bright, sunny day is perfect for his video calls, but cloudy days send him to another part of the house which may be occupied by other family members. And beware of the havoc daylight savings time plays on your carefully calibrated lighting setup! I've seen people slowly fade into darkness during a call that went unexpectedly long when the clocks changed.

PRO TIP:

Define a backup plan for various types of lighting situations and check your lighting (and the weather forecast!) before each call as part of your preparation.

Artificial Lighting Guidelines

If you don't have access to adequate natural lighting, artificial light can be used to either enhance what sunlight you have by balancing out any shadowed areas or take over completely.

Like natural light, the light source should still be positioned in front of you. The types of lights you use can vary, but keep in mind that the larger the light source, the better job it will do of evenly dispersing light on your face. It takes some experimenting to achieve the same even effect natural lighting produces with artificial lighting. Below are some guidelines:

- **Experiment with the lights you have.** Often, replacing harsh white bulbs with softer LED bulbs with a high CRI (Color Rendering Index) may make them useable for video.
- **Videographers swear by the three-point light set up: one key light in front of you and one slightly smaller light on either side of you to cancel out the shadows.**
- **Consider a ring light with a dimmable feature.** The ring nicely illuminates your face and can be adjusted for a variety of less-than-perfect lighting conditions.

PRO TIP:

Getting streaks of light across your screen? It may not be your lighting. You may just need to clean your camera lens!

Help for the Bespectacled

If you wear glasses, you've likely noticed a persistent glare or reflection of your light source appearing in your lenses on video. Here are some tricks that may minimize this problem, starting with the least expensive:

- **It's easy to forget that your monitor is also a light source.** Dimming it often reduces glare immediately.
- **Adjust the angle of your light source downward slightly or move the light away from your face.**
- **Raise the earpieces on your glasses so that they tilt down to avoid catching that glare.**
- **Add side lighting to balance out the main source of light.**
- **Go to the source of the problem and invest in a pair of non-glare glasses.**

Wardrobe

What you wear communicates a lot to your virtual audience very quickly. It's part of your first impression and right or wrong, people make assumptions about you from what is visible to them. As with a face-to-face meeting, you want to appear at your best and most professional on video. I'm going to assume you know what that means in terms of wardrobe for your industry, age, and audience. What you may not know is what your choice of clothing communicates to your audience. Many people are unaware of how the camera reads certain elements like, light, color, and depth, or how the camera frame impacts your audience's perception of your appearance.

Here are some things to consider when choosing what to wear for a video call:

The Neckline Is Everything.

Most of us have never thought about necklines in isolation. We tend to evaluate ourselves in terms of the entire outfit. But in a medium close-up, your audience does not see your entire outfit. In addition, since your neckline frames your face (the focal point on your customer's screen) the neckline plays an oversized role in how your audience perceives you. Here are some tips for finding the best neckline for you on video:

- **No matter how much you paid for it, shirts with a crew neck or t-shirt neckline appear more casual than those with a collared neckline.** For a more professional appearance, pair more casual necklines with a jacket or sweater.
- **Know your most flattering neckline.** If you have a short neck or a stocky build, a crew neck may make you look closed in. In this case, slightly lower jewel necklines (a rounded style that circles the base of the neck and falls above the collarbone) or V-shaped necklines may be more flattering.
- **Lower necklines or off-the-shoulder tops may give the impression that you are revealing much more than you really are, so proceed with caution.**

Colors and Patterns Matter.

The right color can make your eyes and face light up on video, while the wrong color can make you look washed out and less expressive. Start with colors that look good on you in person, then narrow it down with these considerations:

- **Look for colors that provide a nice contrast to your background.** Because the camera doesn't do a good job of reading depth, clothing that is too similar in color to that of your background will cause you to blend right in with it. *(This is another reason why more neutral backgrounds are a good choice. They give you more color options to play with.)*
- **Bright colors tend to make your face pop.** Jewel tones, like blues, teals, greens, or pinks warm up most faces in a flattering way.
- **Beware of black.** I know this will send many of you screaming to your closets *(it did me!)*, but black receives mixed to poor reviews on video. While great for contrast with a white or light background, black limits depth perception, so unlike the slimming effect that black has in person, it can make you look like a shapeless lump on video. If you choose to wear black *(and I know some of you*

will!), always ensure it's well-fitted.

- **Nude colors may make you look... well... nude!** Be sure that there is enough saturation and texture in your nude-colored clothing that no mistakes may be made.
- **Bright reds and whites are known to cause technical problems on camera.** The reds may bleed, causing a fuzzy or halo effect, and whites can glow unnaturally. A touch of white under a jacket or sweater, however, doesn't present those same problems and can add some needed contrast.
- **Avoid stripes and checks, if possible, as they may buzz (i.e., appear to move) on camera**. Larger patterns look great when seen in the bigger picture, but they can appear overwhelming and steal focus from your face in the small frame of video.
- **Limit accessories to one or two.** A simple necklace or pair of earrings is often enough to show personality or add polish. Avoid shiny or sparkly jewelry *(put away that three-carat diamond!)* and opt for accessories with a matte finish. Avoid jangly bracelets or anything that will make a sound when you move or accidentally bang it against your desk.
- **Be consistent.** Part of establishing credibility is being consistent and that consistency should extend to how you show up for your customer. You don't want to wear a three-piece suit one day and show up in a wrinkled t-shirt the next.

When In Doubt, Test It Out!

Always try clothes and accessories on in front of the camera before you get on a video call or do a recording. During your test, make sure you have the actual lighting that will be present during a call. Take a screenshot of yourself and review your choices objectively. Is the color flattering? Is there anything that could cause a distraction to your audience, e.g., accessories that reflect the light, or large prints that dominate the screen? As the only view of you that your audience will have, does it accurately convey the image you desire?

In addition to appearance, it's also important that you're comfortable in what you wear. Just as you wouldn't wear a new pair of shoes for the first time for an in-person presentation, never wear a piece of clothing or an accessory for the first time on a video call. Something as simple as a forgotten tag or a floppy sleeve might drive you (or your audience) crazy during your call and keep you from focusing on the conversation.

PRO TIP:

Get yourself some clothespins. Production crews order them by the carton because they're so versatile on set. They're great for gripping cords, cables, and more without getting hot. And they're perfect for clipping extra fabric to make your clothes fit just right on video. Just keep in mind that if you move, your audience may see your nifty trick!

Makeup

Using makeup to appear on video is not about vanity. Every actor appearing on camera—even those who normally don't wear makeup—needs some makeup to correct the distortions caused by lighting and lenses. Today's high-definition cameras are especially unforgiving in their magnification of flaws. Lights can wash out your skin tone and cause faces (and heads) to shine and reflect light unnaturally. While these imperfections may not bother you, they may bother and distract your audience.

Luckily, you don't need to invest in a ton of new makeup or learn a whole new routine to look awesome on video. The rule is to keep it simple and natural. Less is more on camera. And, of course, all of the special makeup in the world will not make up for poor lighting, so first and foremost, make sure your lighting is set up as mentioned earlier.

Following are a few tips on what to look for and how to apply makeup for video calls by commercial makeup artist Becky Laschanzky, who has worked on film, video and television sets for years.

- **Foundation.** A good foundation that closely matches your skin tone can even out your complexion and sometimes reduce shine. Look for a foundation that is not too matte or too shiny. A liquid or creamy stick, like Maybelline Fit Me, is a good, inexpensive choice.
- **Concealer.** Lighting often casts shadows under your eyes and magnifies blemishes. A concealer one shade lighter than your foundation can often offset this effect.
- **Powder.** If you only use one item of makeup on video, let it be powder. As mentioned above, both lighting and high temperatures can make your face or head shiny, thus drawing undue attention and making you appear nervous. Use a translucent powder and go light. Too much may appear cakey and reinforce lines.
- **Bronzer.** A medium tone matte bronzer is great for adding contour since video flattens your face out. Bronzer is especially helpful if you are located in a bright room or if artificial lights wash you out. Apply where the sun would naturally hit the face, e.g., forehead, tops of cheeks, across the bridge of the nose.
- **Highlighter.** A matte powder or cream highlighter can add light to areas of your face that are typically in the shadows on video, like the inside corner of your eyes and the outer corners of your mouth. Look for something in a light pink or beige tone and apply sparingly.
- **Eye Shadow.** Your eyes should be the first thing your audience sees when you are on video. To highlight them, use a matte shadow in neutral tones. Avoid bright-colored or sparkly eyeshadows, as they will draw attention to themselves. Be sure to blend any shadow in well, as any lines may appear harsh on camera.
- **Eyeliner.** Eyeliner can really make your eyes pop on video, especially if you wear glasses. Use dark brown, charcoal grey, or soft black to add contrast and depth to eyes. For a more natural look, Becky suggests only using eyeliner on top lid and tapering the line from ultra-thin on the inside corner of the eye to slightly thicker on the outside corner of the eye.

- **Mascara.** Black mascara is great for providing contrast and making your eyes look wider and more awake.
- **Eyebrow Pencil.** Brows frame the eyes and add a polished, professional look. We often use our eyebrows to indicate emotions like interest, surprise, or concern. These emotions can get lost on video and disappear under artificial lighting if you have exceptionally light or sparse eyebrows. A brow pencil one shade lighter than your natural brow color can give your brows more substance.
- **Lipstick or Tinted Lip Balm.** After your eyes, the mouth is the second thing most viewers look at on video. Softer matte shades in neutral pinks, corals, or mauve can add a fresh pop of color and take years off your face. Beware that very light nudes, or any lipstick shades that are lighter than your natural lip color can turn chalky on video. If you don't use lipstick, try a soft pink lip gloss on top of a nude lip to add color and avoid looking washed out on camera.
- **Blush.** Yes, blush is different than bronzer! Applying a pink or coral blush to the apple of your cheeks gives most people a splash of color and a more youthful look.

Hair

Hairstyles come and go *(and come back again)*, but whatever your style, make sure that it allows your audience to see your face. Avoid hairstyles that require you to constantly brush hair out of your eyes or tuck loose strands behind your ears. Movement on video is highly visible to your audience and movement near your face is doubly so.

Take care with popular messy hairstyles. While they may look professional in person, their messiness is magnified by the camera and can take you from fashionable to frumpy in a hurry as the camera and lighting shine a spotlight on flyaway hairs. Tame some of those wisps by spraying hairspray or squeezing a bit of styling gel in your hands, rubbing your hands together, and lightly patting down those hairs until they behave.

Don't forget about facial hair. *(And no, I'm not talking about adding facial hair with a filter!)* Remember, your audience is sitting the equivalent of two feet away from you with often only your face to view. Wild hairs, whether they're coming from your eyebrows, nose, ears, or upper lip are more visible on camera and may need pre-meeting attention.

EXERCISE

REVIEW YOUR STAGE

Take a screenshot of yourself looking directly at the camera in the actual lighting, clothing, and makeup you will be using for your video call or recording. Ask yourself or a trusted peer or friend:

Am I framed well? Do I appear to be looking myself in the eye?

Am I showing enough of my torso to avoid that floating head look?

Is there a fist-sized space between the top of my head and the frame?

Is my lighting adequate? Are there any shadows on my face or am I over lit?

Is my background neat and supportive? Are there any distractions I need to eliminate?

Does my clothing convey the impression I desire? Does the color contrast well with my background and complement my face and eyes?

Is my face shine-free? Is my face washed out? Do I need some additional contour? Are my real eyes drawn to my screen eyes?

Is my hair neat and out of my eyes? Is there any unwanted hair visible?

CHAPTER 5

THERE'S MORE TO EYE CONTACT THAN MEETS THE EYE

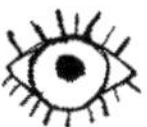

In theater, the primary tool for me was voice.
On-screen, it's the eyes.

JEFFREY WRIGHT, ACTOR

Have you ever watched a movie or television show and felt like the actor on screen was talking to you? I mean, actually seeing you through the screen and speaking directly to you?

The first time I experienced that I was watching *Ferris Buehler's Day Off.* When Matthew Broderick (pretending to be sick to stay home from school) suddenly bolted upright in bed, looked me in the eye, and declared "They bought it!" after his parents closed the door, so did I. It wasn't until many years later that I learned he was using a camera technique called "breaking the fourth wall." You may have seen this technique more recently in television shows like, *Modern Family* or *The Office*, or movies like, *Fight Club* or *Deadpool.* And like me, you may have become instantly more engaged.

Breaking the Virtual Fourth Wall to Connect with Your Audience

The fourth wall is an imaginary wall that separates and distances the actor from the audience.[xxii] When an actor breaks through the fourth wall or speaks directly to the camera, it creates a personal connection between you and the actor. It makes you feel like you are engaged in a one-on-one conversation with them, instead of the way you usually watch a film, which is as a more passive observer.

We have that fourth wall with our customers now too, in the form of a screen. Sellers routinely reinforce that wall by ignoring the camera and staring at their screens, thus separating themselves from an already unresponsive virtual audience. Wouldn't it be powerful if you could break through that wall and create the same personal connection with your customer as those actors do with each member of their audience? In this chapter, you will learn just how to do that whether you're talking to one person or one thousand, and regardless of whether they have their own camera on or not.

BEHIND THE CAMERA

Breaking the Fourth Wall in Film and TV

There you are comfortably snuggled into your couch watching a movie when suddenly the main character seems to look past the camera, directly at you, and begins speaking to you. This theatrical technique called breaking the fourth wall originated in live theater but has become a popular device used in film, television, and even video games. Here are some popular examples of breaking the fourth wall that you may recognize:

- **House of Cards:** Kevin Spacey's character Frank Underwood often addresses the camera to let the audience in on his schemes. Unsettling, to say the least.
- **The Wolf of Wall Street:** Leonardo DiCaprio as former stockbroker Jordan Belfort confesses to the audience how a nice guy like him got in over his head. It almost made me feel sorry for him...
- **Ferris Buehler's Day Off:** Matthew Broderick as Ferris talks directly to the audience throughout the film, even scolding them for staying through the credits at the end.
- **Goodfellas:** During the dramatic courtroom scene, Ray Liotta suddenly stands up in the witness box and walks up to the camera to tell his side of the story while everyone else in the scene freezes. Captivating.
- **High Fidelity:** The audience plays therapist to John Cusack as he tries to figure out where he went wrong in past relationships. (I have some ideas!)
- **Kiss Kiss, Bang, Bang:** Robert Downey Jr. gives a master class on how to break the fourth wall, right up to thanking the audience for coming at the end.
- **Modern Family:** Part of the hilarity of this Golden Globe winning series are the mockumentary-style interviews the characters have with the camera.

Why Eye Contact Matters on Video

If you are not looking at the camera,
you are not connecting with your audience.

JULIE HANSEN

Imagine meeting a friend in person to discuss a situation that has been weighing heavily on you, and your friend constantly breaks eye contact with you to scan the room or check their phone. Would you feel like opening up? Or would you be more likely to feel hurt, ignored, or even annoyed?

Think back to a live meeting where the presenter rarely took their eyes off their slides. Did you feel engaged and connected? Or did you find yourself tuning out, watching the clock, or stealing glances at your phone?

It's no different on video. These are the same feelings that your customer experiences when you fail to look them in the eye—via your camera—on video. Here are some research-backed benefits for making eye contact on video a priority:

Fast Track Relationships

Eye contact is one of the quickest and most effective ways to connect with another person and build a relationship.[xxiii] You can certainly build a relationship without it, but it takes much longer to establish the trust and credibility that sufficient eye contact quickly affords. Desperate to connect yet not looking at the camera is like a drowning person passing up a life raft because it's less comfortable than their couch.

Improve Credibility

The eyes are the windows to the soul is an expression well over five hundred years old, but like many an old adage, it contains the seeds of truth. We often look into the eyes of another person to verify that they are telling the truth. Research indicates that approximately two-thirds of the population believe that people avert their eyes when they are lying or feel guilty.[xxiv] The fact that this same research has shown that eye contact is not necessarily a reliable indication of deception doesn't matter. Perception is reality. Holding someone's gaze makes you appear more believable and trustworthy.

Project Confidence

Looking someone directly in the eye projects confidence.[xxv] Leaders and people with higher status tend to make more eye contact, while trouble meeting a person's gaze indicates an insecurity that the sender may or may not feel.

Convey Likability

All things being equal, people do business with people they like. And people are considered more likable and friendly when they deliver a direct gaze. Not just a fleeting gaze either. Likability increases with the duration of their gaze.[xxvi]

Four Types of On-Screen Eye Contact

Despite the many benefits associated with direct, consistent eye contact, a shockingly small percentage of people are making enough or the right kind of eye contact with their audience while on video. Eye contact (or lack of eye contact) by sellers on video calls or meetings currently falls into one of the following four categories:

1. **The Screen Starer**
   Whether looking at a customer's image, reading from slides or notes, or managing their platform or content, the Screen Starer is A) not meeting their customer's eyes and B) looking down, with all the negative qualities associated with both. The Screen Starer often feels very strongly that they are making eye contact when looking at their customer's image. I have had to crush this magical belief for many disappointed salespeople.

2. **The Close, But No Cigar Speaker**

   If you and I were having a face-to-face conversation and my eyes were focused an inch to the right of your right eye, you'd probably start to get self-conscious, wondering if you had a loose piece of hair sticking up or if someone was creeping up behind you. Most people don't realize how precise the camera's focal point is and how clearly it reads the direction of your eyes. This is partly due to humans obviously visible whites of the eye (or sclera) making the irises so much more prominent. Unlike other animals with tinted or nonvisible sclera, it is easy to tell fairly accurately where a person is looking.[xxvii]

   When your gaze is even just slightly off, it can be nearly as distracting to your observer as if you were looking down. This indirect gaze often occurs because people have not nailed down the exact location of their camera lens (common with iPad and laptop camera users) or they feel like the customer's image is close enough to their camera to get away with it. Close, but no cigar.

3. **The Darter**

   The Darter flips their focus back and forth between camera and screen, camera and screen, trying to cover all their bases. Shifty or erratic eye movement is closely associated with a guilty conscience or fabricating information. Again, these are not qualities you want popping into your customer's head.

4. **The Deer in the Headlights**

   These are people who may technically be looking at the camera but appear to be gazing into a black abyss. Their eyes convey direction, but no meaning, emotion, or intention. In this area, the camera is unforgiving in its perspective. While certainly a beginning has been made, there is still much to do to create that friendly, personal gaze that makes your customer feel like they are sitting across from you having a chat.

Why Is It So Difficult to Look at the Camera?

You don't need instruction on making eye contact with someone who is standing in front of you. So, you may find it quite perplexing that a skill that you've been performing without much thought or effort until now is suddenly so awkward and challenging. But there are some clear reasons why you may find looking at the camera a struggle:

- **To quote Lady Gaga, "Baby, you were born this way!" The human face is one of the most compelling images to another human being.**[xxviii] And because of how you are wired, no matter how much you try to look at the camera, you may find yourself repeatedly drawn to that surrogate image of your customer on your screen—unless you have another way to read your audience and a strong technique to counter this urge.
- **Camera/eyes misalignment.** Most people's cameras don't line up with the image of their customer on their screen. You can, and should, move your customer's image around on your screen to match up as close to the camera as possible, but it likely will not be a perfect match. And, as people join or leave your meeting, their images will shift. However, it's disruptive (to you and your audience) to continually move your camera every time that happens. Even as technology delivers smarter and more flexible cameras, you can't rely on perfect alignment of eyes and camera.
- **It feels like the real deal.** Like the Screen Starer, your mind may trick you into thinking that if you focus intently enough on your customer's face on your screen, they will surely be able to tell you are making eye contact! It doesn't, and they won't.
- **Letting go of cues.** Good salespeople are adept at picking up those little cues or tells from a customer's face and body language to gauge understanding, engagement, interest, or concern. The thought of letting go of that input and turning their attention to the camera leaves them feeling lost and unanchored.

- **Intensity.** Seldom do we stare at a single point for an extended time. Even when we are watching a television show or movie, we are taking in the full screen, not one small section of it. It feels restrictive. You may even have grown up in a household where you were forced to stare at a wall for an uncomfortable length of time as punishment! It is not easy to keep your attention on such a narrow focal point and be engaging, dynamic, and animated.
- **Everyone else looks at their screen.** Yes, they do. However, as you may have been told as a child, just because everyone else is doing it doesn't make it right. In fact, in a worldwide web full of bad eye contact, making great eye contact is a major differentiator and will give you a significant advantage in a crowded field.

Excuses Don't Matter.

If you're not looking at the camera, you're not actively connecting with your customer. Excuses and good intentions score you no points on video. If you're looking down, your customer doesn't know what you're looking at (unlike in person) and you are breaking your connection. Not only that, there are negative associations to looking down, like submissiveness or uncertainty, that you're wise to avoid in any relationship.

You can argue the above points all you'd like, but it doesn't change the fact that if you are not looking into the lens of the camera, despite the challenges associated with that effort, your customer is likely to feel that you're distracted or uninterested in them.

The bottom line is this: Unless you are looking directly at the camera lens, you are not making eye contact with your audience, and you are limiting your ability to develop a meaningful relationship.

Creating Personal Eye Contact

By now, I trust I've made it abundantly clear that you need to look at the camera. What is probably unclear is how to do it in a way that feels natural and allows you to read body language, check or take notes, or share slides or content on video. Lucky for us, actors, broadcasters, and others have grappled with this challenge for decades and provide a helpful roadmap for successfully creating personal, friendly eye contact on camera. I have taught this technique to thousands of people all over the world. Of all the techniques I teach, this one produces the most amazing results. Not only does it make your audience feel more seen and heard, but they're also likely to be more responsive. And for you the speaker, it provides a sense of ease and confidence by creating a more natural and fluid conversational dynamic.

The first thing to know about speaking to a camera is that there is no such thing as talking to a group of people. Eye contact on video is very personal. No matter how many people are on your call or in your meeting, you are still only talking to one person. That is because each person is having their own individual experience and connection with you. When you are (or imagining you are) speaking to an individual, your focus is much tighter, your gaze more intimate, and your body language specific and less presentational. When you are talking to a group, your eye contact is more impersonal and less focused; your movements are often larger and broader. People know the difference, even if it's on a subconscious level.

This personal level of eye contact is precisely how Ryan Reynolds, as *Deadpool*, your Peloton instructor, or your favorite YouTube guru addresses thousands or even millions of people at the same time and makes each individual feel like they are engaged in a private conversation with them. The beauty of this technique is that it doesn't matter whether you can actually see the person you're talking to, or you have to picture that person in your mind's eye. The experience of that individual connection will be the same for each person in your audience.

The "Act As If" Method

Creating personal eye contact starts by visualizing one person, followed by the "Act As If" technique. Actors use this technique to mentally replace a negative or neutral object or person with a positive one. This changes the actor's attitude and actions, stimulates an emotional connection with the other person, and helps them to envision their audience or scene partner when they can't see them. Many successful broadcasters and connectors employ this technique on-camera, often without realizing it. They just know it works!

BEHIND THE CAMERA

Legendary American sportscaster Jim Nantz shares how he uses the Act As If technique to create that one-on-one conversational experience with an audience of sometimes millions: "The late, great ABC golf anchor Jim McKay once advised me, 'When you look into the camera, imagine that you are talking to one person on the other end.' The next time you hear 'Hello, friends' at the start of a broadcast, know that I'm channeling my father at that moment. I see him on the other side of that camera, smiling right back."

Acting As If can repair that broken communication loop by allowing you to "see" your audience and engage in a dynamic conversation—whether your customer has their video on or not. Here are the steps involved:

1. **Mentally project an image of an individual onto the lens of the camera.**
2. **Imagine that person's reactions as you speak.** This can include body language, facial expressions, and small verbal acknowledgments, like *hmm* or *uh-huh*.
3. **Respond to these perceived reactions in real-time, thus closing the communication loop.**

Let's break down each step so you can see how you might apply this on video calls, meetings, and recorded messages:

STEP 1: Project Your Customer's Image onto the Camera Lens

Too many presentations or pitches are just a string of words spoken into the air. By clearly identifying and visualizing your customer in your mind's eye, and then projecting that image onto the camera lens, you immediately connect with your message and your audience in a more personal and specific way. Gone are the obvious blank eyes and the deer in the headlights stare. Your customer—and everyone else on the call—will feel like you are looking at them, seeing them, and speaking to them. That will make them feel like they are actively involved in the conversation rather than passively observing from the sidelines.

STEP 2: Visualize Your Customer's Reactions

One of the biggest complaints I hear from sellers and executives alike about being on video is that they feel like they're talking to themselves. Why? Most of those small but meaningful nonverbal signals that indicated that people heard or understood you, like a nod of the head or a change in expression, are gone. Either your customer has their video off, you're looking at the camera, or your customer has adopted a stalwart poker face that provides you with zero clues as to what they are thinking or feeling. Even those small verbal reactions, the murmured *uh-huh* or *hmm* are often missed on video.

This is the broken communication loop in action. A message is sent but there is no confirmation on whether your customer received it or interpreted it correctly. Your choices seemingly are to proceed blindly on *(which is uncomfortable)*, or continually ask for confirmation *(which makes you appear needy and uncertain to your audience and quickly becomes annoying)*.

Without any reactions from a customer, even the most thick-skinned seller may assume the worst: the customer is not interested, they're impatient, bored, irritated. This interpretation often causes the seller to speed up, cut out some sections of their pitch, or eliminate all pauses. In so doing, the salesperson turns their fears into reality, all because the salesperson is not getting the feedback that they would expect to receive when meeting that customer face-to-face.

Would you like to stop that chain of negative consequences from happening and keep the communication loop intact? You can—and you don't even need your customer's help. All you have to do is imagine what your customer's reaction would be to what you are saying.

Monologue vs. Dialogue

No sales conversation, pitch, presentation, or speech is truly a one-sided monologue delivered in a vacuum. Even a recorded video is not a monologue; it's a dialogue. You are always speaking to someone and feeding off their real (or imagined) reactions to what you're saying. This is how great actors breathe life into a monologue. They are imagining their scene partner's verbal or nonverbal reactions to their words and reacting accordingly. This is what creates a dynamic dialogue despite being unable to see your audience or generate a response from often unexpressive virtual audiences.

Let's look at a famous monologue and see how a great actor might use this technique to bring a short monologue to life by responding to his silent (and perhaps unseen) scene partners. Here is Jack Nicholson's monologue from *A Few Good Men*:

"You can't handle the truth! Son, we live in a world that has walls, and those walls have to be guarded by men with guns. Who's gonna do it? You? You, Lieutenant Weinberg? I have a greater responsibility than you can possibly fathom. You weep for Santiago, and you curse the Marines. You have that luxury. You have the luxury of not knowing what I know—that Santiago's death, while tragic, probably saved lives; and my existence, while grotesque and incomprehensible to you, saves lives…" [xxix]

You may wonder how this could be a dialogue, after all, Nicholson is the only one talking. He begins by focusing on speaking to one person, (Tom Cruise), and while Cruise doesn't have any lines yet, he and the other actors in the scene are certainly reacting to what Nicholson says, which feeds Nicholson's next line.

Now, let's assume that Cruise and the rest of the actors are not even on the set when Nicholson has to shoot his part of the scene (as is often the case). In order to deliver a forceful and believable performance, Nicholson has to see Cruise in his mind's eye (Step One). Then he imagines Cruise's reactions (Step Two). And finally, he responds to those reactions (Step Three). Here's how that might look in practice:

"You can't handle the truth!" (Nicholson imagines Cruise's shocked silence. In response, Nicholson starts explaining the situation, as if to a child): "Son, we live in a world that has walls, and those walls have to be guarded by men with guns. Who's gonna do it? You? You, Lieutenant Weinberg?"

(Nicholson imagines Cruise and team balking at the idea of stepping up to this responsibility. Energized after feeling he has scored a point, Nicholson continues): "I have a greater responsibility than you can possibly fathom."

(Nicholson imagines Cruise repulsed by this revelation, sparking Nicholson's righteous indignation): "You have the luxury of not knowing what I know—that Santiago's death, while tragic, probably saved lives; and my existence, while grotesque and incomprehensible to you, saves lives..."

Nicholson is not just spouting words into thin air; he is working off perceived reactions from his scene partner, which adds depth, and meaning, and emotion to his words, and contributes to an Oscar-winning performance.

STEP 3: Respond to Perceived Reactions

While it's unlikely you will have a conversation with your audience as heated as the previous example *(hopefully!)*, you can use this same approach to turn any potential monologue into a dialogue.

For example, let's say you're sharing good news with your customer, who is not on video:

"We've added a feature that allows you to target messages based on interests, in addition to roles, so you don't have to do it manually anymore." (You imagine your customer smiling, nodding, or murmuring, *hmm* or *cool*...! Your reaction to this is to smile and continue your story with even greater energy and confidence).

Responding to an expected reaction (one you are fairly certain your message would elicit from your customer) completes the communication loop. It provides you with the necessary energy and motivation to continue.

How Do I Know How My Customer Will React?

Every customer is unique, but people aren't as unpredictable in their reactions as you may think.[xxx] Yet in the absence of seeing or hearing any verbal or non-verbal reactions from our audience, we assume we have no idea what they're thinking, or we tell ourselves horrible, worst-case scenarios. This is nonsense if you look at it objectively. You have years or experience communicating with people. How often have they truly surprised you with an unexpected response? For example, if you share a humorous anecdote with a customer in person, you might expect them to smile or perhaps roll their eyes good-naturedly. If you share something interesting (again, in person), your customer might cock their head, widen their eyes, or lean forward. It would be extremely unlikely in either case that your customer would have a significantly different reaction, right? *(Unless your joke was off-color, or your "interesting" idea was yesterday's news.)*

Believing every conversation is going to be full of unexpected and unpredictable reactions keeps us from confidently engaging in a two-way conversation. Unless you've said something controversial, astonishing, or challenging *(like, "You can't handle the truth!")*, your customer is most likely going to respond as anticipated. Just because you can't see their reaction (their video is off or you're not looking directly at them) does not mean they aren't reacting as you'd expect.

Responding to expected reactions allows you to deliver your next thought, question, or statement with the same energy, intonation, and timing as you would if engaged in an active dialogue. By closing the communication loop and focusing on this natural give and take of a conversation, you create a fluid exchange that feeds you and draws in your audience. You're not rushing through it as if your customer is bored and dying to get off the call. Your eyes aren't darting around to check if anyone is paying attention. *(They'll be looking at their screens anyway!)* You are committed to a conversation with your customer as surely as if they are seated across from you. Acting as if you received a response from your customer will energize and motivate you and make a world of difference in how your customer responds to you.

You may still be concerned about how a customer is going to react to what you've said. After all, you're not 100 percent certain of their reaction, right? Yet, there's little downside to imagining the best possible response from your customer. Why? Because it will bring out the best in you. Your energy will be positive and contagious. Your face will be more expressive, your eyes will sparkle, and your tone will inspire, reassure, or intrigue, as needed. Conversely, imagining the worst possible reaction brings out all of the negative characteristics previously mentioned. By responding to perceived positive feedback you are more likely to generate that perceived response in your customer, and you may even change a customer from a negative to a positive state.[xxxi]

An Example of Acting As If:

(Me: to camera) "This report shows you all of the key metrics of your workforce in one place, in real-time."

(Me: Imagining that the client is cocking their head in interest, I continue, encouraged): "Not only that, but you can drill down into each metric to find out the details behind it, information that previously took you days and weeks to collect.

(Me: picturing the client widening their eyes in interest. I nod in response, gaining momentum): "So, you can see how this will help you to be more proactive and accurate in making decisions."

When You Absolutely, Positively Need to Look at the Camera

You want to aim for making eye contact—via the camera—with your customer about 80 percent of the time. You've probably done the math and realized that means you can break eye contact with your customer up to 20 percent of the time. This "free time" can be used to gather your thoughts, check notes, transition from slides, check on listener body language, etc. (More on this in Chapter 11.) Just know that there are certain times in particular when your eyes absolutely, positively need to be on the camera, such as when you are:

1. **Delivering a key point.** Your value proposition, benefit statement, or competitive differentiator will be much more memorable and credible if you look into your customer's eyes (the camera) as you are delivering it.
2. **Asking a question.** If I asked you a question while looking down at my screen, you'd likely be uncertain whether I expected you to answer it. If multiple people were on the call, you might assume my question was directed to someone else. The simplest way to exponentially improve the chances of receiving a response to your question is to look directly into the camera as you ask it, holding your gaze there until you receive an answer.
3. **Listening to your customer.** I know how counter-intuitive this seems! You want so badly to look at your customer's image on your screen because you think it will make them feel heard. Unfortunately, looking at your screen has the opposite effect on your customer. To make your customer feel heard, you need to look at the camera when they speak. But rest assured you will

learn how to combine maintaining good eye contact with reading body language in the next chapter.

The One Person with Whom to Avoid Making Eye Contact

There is one person on a video call with whom you do NOT want to make eye contact. This person will instantly sever the connection between you and your customer and cause you to lose your concentration and confidence. Who is this fickle foe? It's you!

It is always obvious to me when a salesperson checks out their own image on video. First, the seller glances down at their screen. This is often followed by some minor physical adjustment (sitting up straighter, tucking a strand of hair behind an ear, or pasting on a sudden and often unrelated smile). When they finally return their gaze back to the camera, it always takes them a few moments to re-focus. Frequently, they end up rechecking themself to see how the adjustment they just made is holding up. It's a bit like trying to see your own shadow.

This is a vicious cycle that takes you right out of the conversation. Not only does it cause you to break eye contact with your customer, but it places your focus on the wrong person... you. And because few people like what they see during those spot checks, it's difficult not to be hyper-critical of yourself. In those few seconds you spent thinking about yourself, you have cut the connection between you and your customer.

The time to check how you look on camera is *before* your customer joins the video call or you hit the record button. Take a screenshot of yourself and review it. Make sure you are lit and framed well, that your hair and appearance pass the test, and that there is nothing in frame that may potentially cause a distraction for you or your audience. And then, let it go. Once you are live, there is no need to check yourself during your call or recording. If you've brushed your hair it will stay brushed, unless you are outdoors or left a window open during a windstorm. Likewise, if you've framed yourself properly, you're not going to disappear out of frame unless you move your chair or your body.

PRO TIP:

It's difficult to resist the siren call of seeing your own image. Most people need an equally powerful deterrent to avoid this temptation. So here it is: Hide your image so that you can't see yourself during the call. Do not turn off your camera! Instead, select the option to hide your image, which is available on most major platforms at this time (including Zoom, GoToMeeting, Webex, and Teams). Hiding your own image eliminates the temptation and allows you to stay in the moment and focus on your audience.

EXERCISE

IMPROVE YOUR EYE CONTACT ON VIDEO BY ACTING AS IF

Think of a customer that you have an upcoming conversation with. Look up their LinkedIn profile and get their picture in your mind. Turn on your camera and hit "record."

Now project their picture into your camera lens. See them in your mind's eye looking back at you, smiling, friendly, happy to see you. Begin talking. When you say something that might elicit a nonverbal response from your customer, imagine them nodding, raising their eyebrows, or leaning forward toward the camera. Let those perceived reactions affect you and motivate you to say your next piece.

Do this for a few minutes, imagining receiving a variety of different reactions from your customer as you speak.

Review your recording.

How was your eye contact?

Was your gaze soft and friendly?

Did your energy or tone change when you responded to your customer's imagined reaction?

When you're ready, try this on a call with friends or family. Remember to picture only one person at a time to make each person feel like you are speaking to them individually.

CHAPTER 6

A NEW WAY TO READ BODY LANGUAGE ON VIDEO

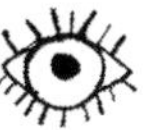

A lot of what acting is, is paying attention."

ROBERT REDFORD, ACTOR / DIRECTOR

Even the most experienced salespeople feel frustrated and impaired when it comes to understanding what their customer is thinking or feeling on a video call. Many of the non-verbal signals that are easily identifiable in person, the nod that meant agreement, the crossed arms that indicated potential resistance, or the raised eyebrows that suggested skepticism, are difficult or impossible to see on video. They're either taking place outside of the camera frame or you're looking at your own camera, slides, notes, or platform tools. And of course, if the customer doesn't have their video on, there's no body language to read!

Welcome to the strange new world of reading body language on video, where little, if any, practical advice currently exists. This gap has left sellers to resort to one of the following ineffective methods:

1. Focus exclusively on the customer's image on the screen, abandoning any attempt to make eye contact.
2. Focus only on the camera, missing any potential nonverbal cues they might receive.
3. Shift focus between the camera and their screen, screen and camera, casting doubt on their credibility or command of the subject.

These are unreliable and often disastrous approaches that limit the seller's understanding of their customer and undermine attempts to build a relationship. In this chapter, you'll learn two methods that allow you to maintain a connection with your customer while getting a big picture read on their attentiveness and interest, as well as picking up subtler movements and expressions at key moments.

Reading Body Language on a Macro Level

Have you ever narrowly escaped colliding with a cyclist or a pedestrian after seeing them out of the corner of your eye? Peripheral vision to the rescue! Your peripheral vision gives you the ability to see objects upon which you are not directly focused. Peripheral vision was an important evolutionary development for humans, allowing us to distinguish between an approaching predator and a potential meal quickly and safely.

Today, most people use their peripheral vision on an as-needed basis, whether it's while crossing the street, skiing down a crowded slope, or navigating a busy grocery store. For those of you who have played any fast-paced sports, like basketball, soccer, or football, you may have relied on peripheral vision to identify open teammates or avoid opponents. But like most people, you probably don't give your peripheral vision much thought the rest of the time. Now is the time to call on this latent skill to help you view your customer's facial expressions and body language on a video call to assess their attention level and interest, without constantly breaking eye contact with them.

Using Your Peripheral Vision to Read Your Customer

Most people have much stronger peripheral vision than they realize. While your sharpest vision is at the center of your gaze, your sight doesn't disappear at the edge of it. Instead, the sharpness and clarity of what you can see decreases gradually the farther you get from your central focal point.[xxxii] This is great news for virtual sellers everywhere! This means that while your eyes are focused on your camera, your peripheral vision should allow you to see major movements or changes in your customer's expression and body language.

To prove this, I often run the following test in my virtual workshops and seminars:

I ask everyone on the video call to focus their gaze on their own camera, not my image. While their eyes are on their cameras, I make a number of movements, gestures, and facial expressions, like tilting my head, crossing my arms, glancing down, or switching from a smile to a frown. Afterward, I ask the participants what they were able to see with their peripheral vision. Ninety percent of them are able to accurately recall every movement or change in expression I made!

In order to access this valuable skill and learn to rely on it, there are a few simple steps you need to take:

1. **Give yourself maximum visibility.** Make sure that you have the largest possible view of your customer on your screen. This will make it easier to use your peripheral vision and increase your accuracy. If you're talking to an individual, choose the speaker view in your platform's video settings instead of gallery view. This way you are seeing only your customer's face on the screen.
2. **Don't focus on yourself.** Hide your image *(remember, you don't need to see yourself!)* or uncheck the box that says, *see myself as active speaker* in Zoom (look for the equivalent in your platform). That will ensure that you have a full view of your customer at all times, not just when they are speaking.
3. **Choose gallery mode for groups.** If you're speaking to more than one person, use gallery mode in Zoom (grid in Webex) to have access to as much of your audience as your screen will allow. Many platforms will enable you to move the gallery images around (you must be in floating view in Webex), placing the video images as close to your camera lens as possible. This will give you the best opportunity to observe your customer's expressions and movements while maintaining eye contact.

4. **Pin your key customer.** If there is one person on your call whose body language is most important to you (e.g., a decision maker), some platforms allow you to "pin" that person's image to a spot near your camera. This allows you to maintain a consistent view of the most important person on your call and not have their image shuffled around your screen every time someone else enters or leaves the meeting.
5. **Focus on the camera.** Once you have set up the images to optimize your peripheral vision, place your central gaze on the camera. With your peripheral vision you should now be able to see changes in the body language and facial expressions of those participants nearest your camera, all while maintaining eye contact with your audience.

Don't be alarmed if the process feels clunky at first. With some practice, you'll come to rely on your peripheral vision to help you read your customer without continually breaking the connection you've worked hard to establish. You'll find a simple exercise at the end of this chapter that will help you develop and improve your peripheral vision.

Reading Body Language on a Micro Level

While your peripheral vision is great for obtaining a general sense of your customer's attentiveness and overall state, there are times where you will want to check in with your customer's actual image on your screen for a more detailed view. Subtler expressions communicated with the eyes and face that may provide a valuable glimpse into your customer's thoughts and feelings may be overlooked by peripheral vision alone. In this case, you may consider doing occasional micro check-ins after these triggering events:

- You've caught a movement, gesture, or expression in your peripheral vision that may indicate a strong emotion, question, or urgency (shaking of the head, furrowing of the brow, leaning toward the screen) that you feel needs to be addressed.

- You notice a repetitive movement, gesture, or expression that indicates the customer may be distracted.
- You've said something controversial or challenging and are uncertain of what your customer's reaction may be.

At these points, you'll want to take a closer look and check in on the customer's actual image on your screen to gain more context. Try to wait until you've finished a complete thought or sentence so as not to look skittish. Once you get your customer in your central focus, quickly determine whether what you see requires further investigation or an adjustment on your part and then return your focus to the camera.

Even without one of these triggering events it's a best practice to do occasional micro check-ins during your call or meeting. While there is no hiding on camera, you can take advantage of opportunities when your customer's eyes are focused elsewhere.

Free Sneak Peek Moments

- **Transitioning between slides or content.** Your customer's eyes will be drawn to this on-screen movement, allowing you a brief moment to take a closer look at their expression and body language.
- **Sharing content.** When you share slides, documents, or software your audience will generally—or at least initially—be focused on those visuals. A couple of caveats: if your slides are simple, your audience will quickly look back to you to provide context, emotion, and meaning to what they've seen. If you look disinterested or appear to be reading from your slides, they may get bored and tune out. I recommend taking a quick look at your audience when you first share content and then returning your focus to your camera.
- **When another speaker is talking to your audience.** If you have deferred the spotlight to someone else (other than your customer), this gives you an opportunity to quickly check out the body language and expressions of your audience in greater detail. Just

remember to bring your focus right back to the camera when it's your turn to speak or if someone is speaking directly to you.

PRO TIP:

Every time you break eye contact with your audience you are breaking your connection. Limit your micro check-ins to no more than once every thirty seconds to avoid appearing shifty-eyed, distracted, or uncertain.

When There Is No Body to Read

In a perfect virtual world, your customer has their video on and you can use your peripheral vision to read their gestures, movements, and expressions while using occasional micro check-ins to fill in the gaps. But we don't live in a perfect world. Customers are not always going to have their cameras on. Recent studies on Zoom Fatigue which chronicle the symptoms of prolonged video conferencing have led some companies and "experts" to suggest limiting video use. While this presents a more significant challenge for you, it is still possible to gain insight and understanding into your customer's interests and attention-level by using the following tips:

- **Brush up on your active listening skills.** Remember using the telephone for more than just texting, taking pictures, or surfing the web? The sound and tone of your customer's voice can provide clues regarding your customer's level of engagement, interest, or understanding. In fact, because people tend to be less physically expressive on video, even if your customer does have their camera on you may be able to tell more from their voice than their face!
- **When your customer speaks, give them your full attention; don't anticipate where they are headed, tune out, or start crafting your response.**
- **Listen to not only what your customer says, but how they say it.** Every word, inflection, and pause provides new information. For example: try saying yes, in the following ways: warmly, impatiently, politely, patronizingly. It's amazing how one word can have so

many different meanings based on the way it is spoken. If the words conflict with the tone, ask yourself what steps may need to be taken to get things back on track. Perhaps you need to provide clarification or an example. Maybe you need to ask them to expand on their response. If something about your customer's response seems incongruent or odd to you, don't just brush it off.

- **Check-in more frequently.** When people know that they are not visible they feel greater freedom to pick up any of the many distractions at their fingertips. Break them of this notion by engaging your customer every two to three minutes (more tips on engagement in Chapter 11).
- **Allow for longer pauses.** Yes, it's uncomfortable to be silent after you ask a question but resist the urge to fly right through those important pauses. You must give your customer enough time to take in your meaning, formulate an answer to your question, and then unmute themselves before forging ahead.
- **Remember that you are still on video.** It's easy to forget that you are still visible when the other people on your call are not. Don't get lulled into thinking you can ease up on your new skills. Work on maintaining eye contact with the camera.
- **Act As If.** Use your imagination to fill in gaps in the communication loop. This will keep your energy up and make the conversation more dynamic. By applying the techniques for making eye contact that you learned in Chapter 5, your customer will feel more comfortable and connected to you.

Finally, don't let the fact that your customer does not have their video on serve as an excuse to turn your video off. The fact that you are visible is to both party's benefit. If you are serious about building a relationship with your customer, your comfort needs to come second. *(Hey, who said sales was fair?)* So, do what you can to encourage your customer to turn their video on, but ultimately, it's more important that you use yours. No excuses.

Peripheral vision, micro-check-ins, and active listening may not provide the amount of information we get from our customer when we are sitting across from them, but they can dramatically improve our current level of understanding while keeping our connection strong. By practicing your peripheral vision (see exercise below) you'll become more adept at it and start to rely on it with confidence.

EXERCISE:
DEVELOP YOUR PERIPHERAL VISION

Find a talking-head video, (*e.g.*, a single speaker or presenter who is framed from the shoulder or chest up and speaking directly to you, the viewer). This will serve to mimic a live video call. Spend a few seconds getting the speaker's face in your mind's eye and then shift your focus to your camera and project the speaker's face onto the camera. Continue to listen to the speaker this way, noting what you can see with your peripheral vision. Check the speaker's image on your screen every twenty to thirty seconds to test your accuracy.

When you're ready, try this on a real call and record it. Did your eyes dart back and forth too much? Did you get stuck looking at certain spots on the screen for too long? Continue to practice this and soon you'll find it comes pretty naturally.

CHAPTER 7

(MIS)INTERPRETING ON-SCREEN BEHAVIOR

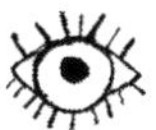

I do not think that means what you think it means.

THE PRINCESS BRIDE

Reading body language on video is like learning another language. While you may recognize the word *no* as a refusal in English, in Czech, it means *yeah*. The body language your customer exhibits on video may not necessarily mean the opposite of what it means in person. Still, there are some common movements and expressions which have a unique meaning on video. For example, if you were in a customer's office and your customer was avoiding eye contact with you or had a disinterested expression on their face, you'd be right to be concerned. But on video? Not so fast. On-screen behavior can be very different from in-person behavior, and you must know the difference to avoid overreacting or underreacting to these signals.

Without any special training in reading body language, you may be a near expert at reading body language in person; after all, you've been doing it all your life. For example, you know that when your partner gives you a certain look at a party that it's time to say your goodbyes. You suspect that when your customer crosses their arms, you may be in for some resistance.

Unfortunately, applying these same in-person interpretations to behavior on video is doomed to failure. In this chapter you'll learn why certain types of on-screen behavior are different from in-person behavior and how to react accordingly so you can avoid needless anxiety, misunderstandings, and failed connections.

Four Reasons Why On-Screen Behavior Is Different Than In Person

1. Receiving Mode

Place the average person in front of a screen and they instantly slip into "receiving mode." It doesn't matter whether that screen is a computer, an iPad, a television, or an IMAX screen. As consumers, we have been primed by media and technology to be passive receivers (for the most part) when in front of a screen, not active participants. Put a bowl of popcorn in front of us and we're ready to sit back and be entertained! This is especially true of customers who are expecting to receive a pitch or a presentation.

Curious what receiving mode looks like? I invite you to jump on any video meeting and take a look at the faces and body language on your screen. How attentive is the body language? How many happy, engaged faces do you see? Look at your own face on a video call. Do you look happy to be there? For most people, the answer is *not really.* This, my friend, is receiving mode—a blank facial expression suitable for high-stakes poker but absolutely useless for reading thoughts or feelings. The only thing this expression tells you is that your listener is alive and awake *(most of the time).*

This expression is so common that I think it deserves its own name. I call it "Resting Business Face" or RBF. Here's an informal definition:

Resting Business Face, or RBF (noun): A deadpan, poker-faced, or impassive expression attributed to, or unconsciously adopted by, a person attempting to be professional during business meetings, video calls, or networking events.

Resting Business Face and other video-specific behavior strikes fear in the hearts of sellers who assign a face-to-face meaning of boredom, impatience, or worse to this blank stare. Sellers resort to numerous self-defeating behaviors when confronted with RBF, like repetitive check-ins or rushing through their pitch or presentation.

This nervousness and discomfort rarely goes unnoticed by the customer *(there's no hiding on video)* and often creates the very feeling the seller has unwittingly projected onto the customer!

2. **Lack of Obligation to Show Interest**

   Most people feel some sense of obligation to maintain a pleasant, interested expression and attentive body language when attending an in-person meeting. Not so *(or not yet)* on video. I am always pleasantly surprised when someone shows up fully present and expressive on video. It indicates some thought, effort, and self-awareness on their part. Sadly, most people are unaware of what their face is communicating on video and unlikely to do anything about it. *(Fortunately, you won't be one of them after you read Chapter 9 on leveraging the power of your expressions.)*

3. **Location-Specific Behavior**

   Seated in an office, surrounded by others, people are less likely to slump, slouch, or look otherwise disengaged than when they are at home. For some, this difference is slight. For others, it is quite dramatic. *(I have resisted the urge to yell, "Sit up straight!" to virtual meeting participants more than a few times.)*

   People tend to let their guard down more at home, which means they are more relaxed and comfortable. And as you learned, this combination can make, not just you, but your audience appear lethargic and uninterested.

4. **Lack of Video Social Skills**

   As much as I'd like this book to get into the hands of everyone who needs it, the reality is that you are among a very select set of people who will have the insight, knowledge, and skills to communicate effectively on video. Most people will remain unaware that their lack of eye contact creates distance between themselves and others. They won't realize that their stony expression causes a speaker to feel anxious and uncertain. While others would certainly benefit from these skills *(and you're welcome to send them this book!)*, it's best not to expect your audience to be adept at them and prepare accordingly with the following strategies.

Five Reinterpretations of Body Language on Video

Fortunately, many nonverbal signals mean the same thing on video as they do when you're face-to-face. For example, people shiver when they're cold, they lean forward when they're interested, and they raise their eyebrows when they're surprised, both in person and on video. But there are some expressions and movements (or lack of expressions and movements) that do possess a unique meaning on video. Being aware of these differences will help you avoid a lot of needless worry and potential misunderstanding.

1. **Resting Business Face**

   (Bored, Disinterested, or Unhappy Expression)

   In its most common form, RBF is a blank stare on video, revealing nothing. At its worst, your customer looks anywhere from mildly to moderately displeased or irritated. The way RBF presents itself on your customer's face has more to do with their own physiology than with how they feel about you and your message. Depending on your disposition, you may react to RBF with a measured, *they're just listening*, to a concerned, *they're bored*, or even a panicked, *they hate me!* The latter two interpretations are likely to throw you well off your game needlessly, as you will see.

   A CASE STUDY IN RBF

   Sonya, an account executive for a busy payroll and benefits company, had finally scheduled an initial meeting with the human resources director at a large retailer and invited her manager to attend. On the video call, the ordinarily cool and collected Sonya found herself rattled by the expression on the HR director's face, which could best be described as utter and complete boredom. Staring at their screens, the rest of the director's team offered little in the way of encouragement either. Halfway through the scheduled meeting, Sonya's manager texted her, "Let's wrap it up. They're clearly not interested." Agreeing with her manager's premise, Sonya stumbled to an awkward finish.

The next day Sonya received an unexpected email from the HR director's assistant asking if they could set up another meeting to discuss how Sonya's company might help them solve their compliance issues. To Sonya's (and her manager's) surprise, the HR director's RBF was not an indication of their level of interest!

The solution to a customer who exhibits Resting Business Face is first and foremost: don't panic. A bored expression on its own does not guarantee boredom on video. Instead, look for clusters of information that support your theory. Is the customer's tone also distant and flat? Do their answers reflect growing impatience? Were they caught off guard when you asked them a direct question? Multiple signals like these may indicate that your customer is not engaged, interested, or has something else pressing on their mind. Then you need to react accordingly.

2. Looking Down

Is your customer looking at your image and engaged, or is their attention elsewhere, like on their email? Short of having surveillance cameras installed in your customer's location, it's impossible to be one hundred percent certain. However, keep in mind that this is how the majority of people communicate on video. Until you read this book, perhaps you too, were guilty of staring at the speaker's image on your screen. Now you know better, but your customer likely doesn't. If your customer is otherwise engaged in your call, they are likely looking at you on their screen.

Cultural differences also can affect the amount and duration of eye contact on video or in person. In Middle Eastern cultures, extended periods of eye contact are the norm, while in certain Asian cultures too much eye contact is often considered rude.[xxxiii]

So how do you know if your customer is looking at your image or doing other work? Here are a few clues that your customer's focus may be elsewhere:

- Their expression is unrelated to what you're saying or what you're sharing on the screen.
- Their eyes are moving left to right repeatedly.
- They are slow to respond or slightly startled when you check in with them.
- They are interacting with someone in their office, off screen.

If, however, your customer is responsive when you check-in, and there is no other suspicious body language, it is fair to assume they are looking at you on their screen. Accepting this as a fact and carrying on as if they are interested and attentive allows you to perform at your best and stay present.

3. **Wandering Eyes**

   This can be a sign of mental or physical distraction, or it could mean your customer is reading, checking email, or waiting for a text. While this is of greater concern than the customer whose eyes are focused steadily down, it's not necessarily a death knell for your call. Your customer may be momentarily curious how others are reacting to what you've shared, someone just passed through their office, or they are simply going back and forth between looking at your image on the screen and their camera. Unless this lasts longer than thirty seconds, occasional wandering eyes are probably not worth disrupting your meeting to check out.

4. **Inattentive Body Language**

   Just as people are less inclined to show attentiveness with their facial expressions on video, the same is true of their body language. That more relaxed posture can make them appear inattentive, even when they are interested. Like eye movements and facial expressions, it's essential to consider all of these elements as a whole, not just individually. For example, if your customer is sitting back, but their smile is warm and authentic, you'd likely be right to assume they are engaged but relaxed.

5. **Moving, Fidgeting, Rocking, etc.**
   While these movements often indicate boredom or disinterest in a face-to-face meeting, on video, they can just as easily mean your customer is restless from sitting on calls all day or has had too much coffee. Keep in mind that many people have repetitive, unconscious movements that may be totally unrelated to what you're saying. These movements are magnified on camera and very easy to obsess over if you let yourself. If these movements are paired with passive facial expressions and poor eye contact, check into it. If they are isolated or habitual movements, do your best to disregard them and carry on as if you have your customer's full interest.

Look for Clusters of Signals

In isolation, most of these expressions, movements, and behaviors are not cause for alarm. If your customer is otherwise engaged and responsive, RBF, poor eye contact, or inattentive body language is likely habitual and unconscious, and has little to do with you, your conversation, or your presentation. However, if your customer exhibits one or more of these signals and is slow to respond or uses a dismissive or disengaged toned, it may be time to take action.[xxxiv]

Handling Inattentive Body Language

Confronting someone on their inattentive body language on video is a little more delicate than in person. In a face-to-face group meeting you might be able to speak louder or stand next to the person you suspect is not paying attention or distracted. Your options are less subtle on video, so it's a good idea to be reasonably sure it's a problem before you risk putting your customer on the defensive.

Before you dive in, make sure you are looking at the camera as you're speaking. If you've forgotten or let up on your eye contact, your audience may feel like they're out of sight, making it easier to drift off without detection. Try engaging in good direct eye contact for a few minutes. This is often enough to solve the attention problem.

If you suspect that your customer has checked out, you may ask, "Am I meeting your expectations for our call so far?" This often breaks that cloak of invisibility your customer may wrongly assume they can hide under.

If the behavior persists, you may want to be more direct and ask, "I can't help but notice that you seem a little distracted. Is there perhaps another task or activity that you need to attend to before we continue?"

Ultimately, you can't control another person's behavior. If you're on a group call, focus on someone who looks attentive as your touchpoint. As most good performers and speakers know, you can't spend all your energy and focus trying to turn one person into a fan to the detriment of everyone else in the audience.

The bottom line on reading your customer's body language on video is this: don't expect customers to react on video as they would in a face-to-face conversation. Understand that things like Resting Business Face, looking down, and inattentive body language are typical on-screen behaviors. Don't allow your over-reaction to these signs to turn into a self-fulfilling prophecy.

EXERCISE

EXPAND YOUR VIDEO BODY LANGUAGE VOCABULARY

To improve your accuracy when it comes to interpreting your customer's body language on video, try this: The next time you're on a video call with a peer, a friend, or a family member, use your peripheral vision, and when you note a change in body language or expression, stop.

Ask your friend or family member what they felt that caused them to smile, lean back, or look at you blankly. Was it the result of what was said, or were they adjusting their position, stretching, or trying to sneak a peek at their phone? Were they even aware that they had a specific expression on their face or moved their body in a certain way? These are valuable insights that will start to expand your video body language vocabulary.

CHAPTER 8

LEVERAGING MOVEMENT AND GESTURES

I'm not sure what to do with my hands.

RICKY BOBBY (WILL FERRELL) IN TALLADEGA NIGHTS

Great body language is any movement or gesture that supports your message by conveying emotion, focus, or context to enhance your audience's understanding and improve recall. Great body language on video rarely stands out. Your customer isn't likely to say, "Boy, her body language was fantastic on that call!" But bad body language—movements or gestures which are unprofessional, repetitive, or distracting—are as hard to ignore as, to quote John Mulaney, "a horse in a hospital."

Whether on video or in person, your body sends out a steady stream of information to your customer, all of which may affect their attention, their perception of your product or service, and their desire to connect with you.[xxxv] Used well, body language makes it easier for your audience to connect with you and allows them to see you as an authentic, caring, and trustworthy human being. The challenge on video is that certain movements and gestures we use face-to-face can hamper that connection and or be easily misread by your audience, causing confusion and misunderstanding. Should we avoid gestures, all together, as some experts would suggest?

"Don't Use Your Hands on Video" Is Terrible Advice.

An executive at a Fortune 500 SaaS company reached out to me for help on improving his video presence. I reviewed a few recordings of Kevin (not his real name) presenting at in-person events in preparation. Dynamic and personable, Kevin walked the stage with ease, connected with his audience, and delivered his message with passion. If Kevin could convey and scale that same energy and enthusiasm on video, I was, quite frankly, unsure how I could help him.

I needn't have worried. I saw no hint of in-person Kevin on our video call. Kevin's delivery was flat as a pancake. His voice was monotone, his face and eyes empty, and the only movement was a repetitive rocking motion back and forth, which made Kevin appear nervous and quickly became my sole focal point.

> After he finished, I asked, "Do you usually use your hands when you talk?"
>
> He laughed. "Oh yes. I always use my hands. It's probably a Jersey thing."
>
> "So why didn't you use them during your presentation?" I asked.
>
> "My last coach told me I shouldn't use my hands on video. He said it was too distracting."

There are many mixed messages floating around regarding how (or how not) to use your hands, arms, and body on video. Gesture! Don't gesture! Act natural! Sit! Stand! Who wouldn't be confused? But recommending that natural gesturers refrain from using their hands to speak on video is terrible advice and almost always produces similar results: ordinarily dynamic, engaging people turn into anemic versions of themselves on video calls by sitting (sometimes quite literally) on their hands.[xxxvi]

When I gave this executive "permission" to use his hands, it was as if he had received a shot of adrenaline. His personality resurfaced, his voice and face were animated, and his passion for his subject was unmistakable. While Kevin's gestures still needed to be finetuned (and that rocking in place reigned in), the simple act of using his hands transformed this executive from a cardboard cutout to a dynamic, engaging, three-dimensional person you could easily connect with.

Body Language and Icebergs

Like an iceberg, ninety percent of your body is invisible to your audience on video. That means your audience is making assumptions about you, your message, and your intentions from the ten percent that they can see. It is critical that this ten percent communicates and reflects your true intent.

The Four Principles for Great Body Language on Video

You've been honing your body language for years but moving and gesturing on video presents some unique challenges, including:

- The "live" area in which you can move or gesture is quite tight.
- The camera distorts some things and magnifies others.
- Your audience is focused very narrowly on a small percentage of your face and body.

Developing effective on-camera body language starts by understanding the following four key principles.

1.
MOVEMENT MUST BE PURPOSEFUL.

The reason for walking is destination!

ARTHUR HOPKINS, DIRECTOR

Like your words and your expression, movement is motivated by a clear purpose. Most people do this quite naturally in face-to-face conversations. For example, you may use your hands to emphasize or clarify a point or to paint a picture for your audience. You may move toward a person in order to engage with them. You may wave your hands to get their attention. A movement starts with a thought, like, *I want to get their attention*, and your body naturally reacts to that thought without you consciously telling it what to do.

Unfortunately, those natural impulses often get lost or drowned out by the nerves or restrictions associated with being on video. This can result in all sorts of unjustified gestures or nervous movements that backfire in their intent. Movements that are disconnected from a clear purpose (in other words, added on for window dressing) ring a false note with your audience every time. Prospects get confused, even suspicious, when your body language doesn't align with what you're saying. This doesn't mean you can't add new movements and gestures to your repertoire, but it does mean that you have to know why you're moving so that your action comes from an authentic starting point.

What's My Motivation to Move?

To find the authenticity in their movements and actions on film, part of an actor's preparation is determining the motivation behind those actions. For example, if a director asked you to walk over to a chair during a scene, you would need to know why you're going there, and the reason would have to make sense to you. Our bodies are purposeful machines. When movement doesn't make sense to us, we often feel self-conscious and awkward. And to our audience, we appear inauthentic or uncertain. This effect is only magnified on video.

Without a clear motivation to move, our body can feel like an unfamiliar suit. *What do I usually do with my arms? How do I normally stand?* It's only once we have a clear reason to move that we feel purposeful and confident.

BEHIND THE CAMERA

This search-for-motivation became a running joke in Hollywood after one earnest actor summoned up the nerve to ask Alfred Hitchcock what the actor's motivation was for taking a particular action in the scene. The famously wry director replied, "Your salary."

Ultimately, it is up to you to find a purpose to move or gesture. That purpose could be internal, e.g., to connect, emphasize, clarify, or share an idea or emotion. Or it could be external, e.g. to show size, demonstrate a movement, indicate distance, etc. If you are clear on your motivation, your body and your gestures often naturally fall into line and support your message. If you are unclear, your movement often confuses your audience and detracts from it.

2.
LESS IS MORE.

Theater acting is an operation with a scalpel, while film acting is an operation with a laser.

SIR MICHAEL CAINE, ACTOR

Have you ever seen a presenter wildly throw their hands around as they speak? While this may be perfectly effective in a live presentation to a large group, those same broad, vague, or fast movements are a primary cause of distraction on video.

In the tight frame of a medium close-up, the camera will pick up even the most subtle gestures and movements. A simple brush of your hand, nod of your head, or finger tap can instantly capture your customer's eye. Large, rapid movements dominate the screen and are often overwhelming and indecipherable to your audience.

While there's no need to control every little movement or eliminate all spontaneity, it's important to be as aware, selective, and precise with your movements as possible to avoid further compromising the already fragile attention span of your audience.

3.
START FROM A STRONG BASE.

You are not a duck.

JULIE HANSEN

Ever notice how ducks paddle furiously underwater while their body above the surface remains perfectly still? I don't know how they do it, but I do know that you are not a duck. Whether sitting or standing in front of the camera, you must have a strong, still base.

Your body is a miraculous collection of interconnected muscles. Moving one body part often causes motion in another part. For example, if you're seated right now, try tapping your foot. You'll notice your knee and thigh begin to shake as well. If you tap with enough force, your upper torso may even get in on the action.

Movement that occurs outside of the camera's frame often results in movement in a body part that is within the camera's frame, and thus, visible to your audience. For example, crossing and uncrossing your legs (out of frame) may cause your torso to shift up and down (in frame). Rocking or swiveling in your chair (out of frame) will cause you to sporadically move closer and farther away from your camera (in frame).

Whether you're moving because you're nervous, your leg fell asleep, or for some deep subconscious reason, it doesn't matter. Your customer will observe and react to the movement. Their reaction may range from a passing curiosity to a complete inability to focus on what you're saying.

Some movements are so distracting or incongruent with what's being said that they call into question your credibility, commitment, or sincerity. I've seen otherwise perfectly competent professionals bounce in their chairs, zoom in and out from a medium to an extreme close-up, wave their arms around frenetically, and basically exhibit the same behaviors as a restless third-grader on video calls. They are giving out loud signals that they do not intend. You can avoid these unforced errors by becoming aware of what your body is doing, how different movements read to your audience on video, and ensuring that every part of your body is in alignment and supporting your conversation, not working against it.

4.
MOVEMENT IS A MAGNET.

There is no hiding on video.

JULIE HANSEN

During my live workshops, I would occasionally have a participant return late from a break. I could be in the middle of sharing the key to instantly tripling your sales, and can you guess what everyone in the room would do when Raj or Karin re-entered? That's right. They would collectively turn their heads toward the door to see someone whom they've sat in class with for an entire day enter the room. Exciting stuff!

The magnetic pull of movement is even stronger on video because of the narrow focus and the fact that there is typically little movement taking place on screen. So, whether you move intentionally or unintentionally on video, your audience will be drawn to that action.[xxxvii] If that action is unrelated to what you're trying to communicate (like rocking in your chair or rubbing your eye), it's extra information that your customer must process and it competes with the message you are trying to communicate. If that movement is repeated, your customer may find themselves unable to focus on anything except your rocking, tapping, or pointing, and they may look for ways to escape.

The Definitive Guide to Using Body Language on Video

Now that you know the principles behind effective body language on video, how and when should you move or gesture? Should your hands rest on your lap or your desk? Should you make big or small movements with your hands? Should they be fast or slow? This problem has plagued actors, sellers, and speakers alike.

Below are some guidelines that will help you start to adapt your face-to-face body language to video.

Know Your Frame.

To gesture well, you must be familiar with the boundaries of your stage. Everything within this area is what the customer will see. Turn on the camera and notice how far you can extend your arms in all directions before they disappear out of frame. Recognize how high you must raise your elbows for your hands to be visible to your audience. You may observe that the area in which your gestures are visible to your audience is quite small. *You can't even extend your arm fully before reaching the edge of the screen! Pointing from the far left of your frame to the far right feels like mere inches!* But don't be fooled. While your movements feel insignificant to you, to your audience they appear quite large.

The goal is to keep as much of your activity within this frame as possible. Any action that cuts your limbs off or references something outside of the frame, reinforces the artificiality of the environment, working against your efforts to create a near in-person experience. This doesn't mean that you can't ever gesture out of frame but try to keep the majority of your movement within it. When your gestures are outside of your frame, your customer misses the full meaning of the gesture, and their brain will try to fill in the gap between what they can and cannot see on video.

If you want to move and gesture clearly and freely within the confines of your stage, you need to develop muscle memory. In other words, you need to know what it feels like in your arms when your hands reach the edge of your frame or how high you have to lift your elbows for your hands to be seen on your customer's screen.

PRO TIP:

Have your video on as you practice your gestures, but don't check your own image to see if you're in frame during a live call. This will come with practice.

Be Precise.

As Sir Michael Caine said, acting on film or video is like operating with a laser. While the consequences of not being laser precise with your movements on video are not as dire as they are in the operating room, precision improves the clarity and impact of your message.

Most people gesture on video the same way they do in person, loosely and ambiguously. But your virtual audience has no context with which to interpret these vague movements. Are you waving your hands across the screen to indicate distance or excitement? Or are you trying to swat a fly or shoo a wandering child out of the room?

On video, the more specific you are with your gestures, the better for your audience. For example, if you're indicating the passage of time, flapping your hands rapidly back and forth in front of you is indecipherable to your virtual audience. Instead, pick the farthest point visible in frame on your right side and place your right hand there. Then, slowly move your right hand to the farthest point you can go on your left while still remaining in frame.

Every movement doesn't have to stay within the lines, but too much generalized movement doesn't improve your message or connection, and more often than not, it confuses your audience.

Eliminate Go-To Moves.

Repetitive gestures are the physical equivalent of crutch words. They're often unconscious, habitual, and compounded by the pressure of being in the spotlight. These go-to moves, whether it's touching your hair, steepling your hands, or rocking back and forth, can quickly become the center of attention for your audience. While these movements may seem minor to you, their repetitive quality gives them outsized significance on the small screen. People are quick to notice patterns *(another handy survival skill!)* and certain members of your audience may start to track repetitive movements, pulling focus away from your message.

Some go-to moves are more noticeable than others. Touching your head, hair, or face is hard to miss since that is your customer's primary focal point. In addition, touching your head makes you appear nervous or uncomfortable. (If you are nervous, be sure to use the recommended tension release exercises in Chapter 2.)

You may be thinking, *I don't have any go-to moves.* That may be, but I encourage you to review a recording or two of yourself and note any unnecessary movements you make and how often you make them. You may simply be unaware of them!

Slow It Down.

You've probably noticed that when someone moves too quickly on camera, things tend to get blurry or you only catch a small part of the movement. This fuzziness *(along with the tendency to lose body parts)* is exacerbated by network connectivity, latency issues, or the use of a green screen or virtual background. Keep your movements slow and deliberate on video unless you are, in fact, making a point about something being fast and unstable. Aim for quality over quantity.

Be Consistent.

Because movement on video is literally "in your customer's face," they will notice not only repetitive movements but inconsistencies in movement as well. For example, if you introduce a sequence of points or steps by holding up the corresponding number of fingers for the first two points, followed by no fingers for point three, and a fist for point four, some members of your audience will notice (and start to track) the discrepancy. Likewise, if you refer to an unseen person, place, or thing as being located on your right, only to later refer back to it as being on your left, it may be both confusing and distracting.

While most of these inconsistencies won't cause a major break in communication, the fact that your customer has to take the time to notice, think about, and finally dismiss them is precious time stolen from your message and the connection you are trying to establish.

Video-Friendly Gestures and Movements

Determining how and when to move on stage or screen is called blocking. While it's not necessary to block out every move you're going to make during a video call or recording, it's helpful to think about places where certain gestures may enhance your connection, convey emotion, or add to your audience's understanding. Below are some places where a gesture or movement could serve your audience and some examples of corresponding video-friendly gestures.

- **To Demonstrate an Action**
  Action words and concepts are natural candidates for gesturing. If you were describing tossing, ducking, or weaving, you would simply make that corresponding movement in frame. You will most likely need to cheat to keep the action within the frame. For example, demonstrating a basketball toss accurately would require most people to extend their arms well beyond the top of their frame. To adapt this to video, simply imagine the basket being located just at the top of your screen. This allows your audience to see the entire movement and better understand what you are trying to illustrate.

- **To Describe a Person or an Object**
  Bringing people, products, and services to life is part of sales, and gestures can help you to do that in a visual way. To indicate someone is tall, for example, you might bring your hand to the top of your screen. This might not seem very tall to you (especially when you're seated), but to your audience, it is as high as they can see, so your point will be clear.

- **To Indicate Change**
  Does your product or service save your customer time, distance, effort, or money? Why not drive that point home with a gesture? For example, you might start with one flat hand at the top of the screen and move it slowly to the bottom of the screen as you say, "This tool helped a customer reduce the amount of time to complete this task from six hours a week to less than one."

- **To Separate Ideas**
  Making sure your audience retains your message is a big challenge on video with the many distractions available to them. One way to ensure all of your points don't blur together is to use your fingers to separate individual points. For example, I might hold up

three fingers when I say, "there are three things I want to address today," and then display the corresponding number of fingers for each point. Be sure to take into account cultural differences. For example, in Germany and France they start counting with the thumb, while in America, we start with the index finger.

- **To Welcome**
  Instead of a handshake, gestures can also convey that you are happy to see your audience. Try bringing your elbows in and opening your palms toward the screen at the bottom of your frame *(remember, open palms help build trust!)* or clasping both hands together in front of your chest as you welcome your participants to the meeting.

- **To Emphasize a Key Point**
  When you feel strongly about a point, it's natural for your body to want to move. This impulse can often turn into vague, large movements which don't read well on video. Instead, convert that energy into smaller, more specific movements. For example, instead of waving your arms around wildly, make a loose closed-fist and pump it in the air on a key point. The karate chop (a flat hand with fingers pointed to the screen or side of your frame) is also an excellent, video-friendly choice for emphasizing certain words or ideas.

- **To Indicate Surprise or Delight**
  Our bodies often move when expressing emotion and we should embrace that urge on video. Try clapping your hands together in front of you (soundlessly, by keeping them rounded), or raising them to your sides from your elbows, with palms open to the ceiling.

- **To Share Gratitude or Emotion**
  Sometimes a verbal, "thank you," or "I'm sorry you're struggling with that," is simply not enough. One way to communicate gratitude, empathy, or any other heartfelt emotion is to use a variation of the "Wakanda Forever" pose from *The Black Panther*,

i.e., crossing both arms in front of your chest. In American Sign Language, this is the symbol for love, but it can also convey support and empathy. If you don't know someone well, I recommend using a single arm and tapping your chest with your fist.

An Example of Blocking

Here's how you might apply video-friendly gestures to a real-world sales conversation.

SALESPERSON

"What I heard you say first," (hold up one finger) "is that you're looking to be able to visualize your entire pipeline." (Place hands together in front of your chest, then simultaneously move both left and right hands to their respective side of the frame.)

CUSTOMER

"Yes, that's correct."

SALESPERSON

"Great. And second," (hold up two fingers) "that you would like to be able to pinpoint what's happening in real-time." (Purse fingers together into a tight cluster.)

CUSTOMER

"Absolutely."

SALESPERSON

"And third," (hold up three fingers) "you want to eliminate as many of those manual processes as possible that are slowing you down today." (Start with hands together on one side of frame, push them slowly to the other side of the frame.)

Note: Don't over-block your movements. If you physicalize and emphasize everything, your main point will get buried, and you risk looking like a bad mime. Blocking is merely a tool to help you think about the possible types of gestures you can use and where they might add meaning and context to your message. But remember, without a clear motivation behind them, gestures can come across as disingenuous and robotic.

WARNING:
Objects May Appear Larger Than They Are

There is another significant perspective issue that you must be aware of when you are working on video. Anything you place close to the camera will look disproportionately large. This includes your hands, your face, your pen, and your wireless presenter. Try moving your hands toward the camera. Notice how enormous they are in comparison with the rest of your body. The same is true of your head. Many people have a habit of leaning their heads toward the camera to connect with their audience. While this is another example of a well-intentioned natural impulse, this puts you in an extreme close-up view, which may come across as aggressive and in-your-face, especially to certain cultures or a new prospect.[xxxviii]

To avoid jarring your customer by lunging toward the camera with your head, torso, or arms, try to maintain an even distance from the camera and keep gestures close to your torso. This is, of course, easier said than done, which is why I developed the "Pane of Glass" technique.

The Pane of Glass Technique

Imagine a pane of glass six inches in front of your face and torso positioned between you and your camera. Your goal is to avoid touching or breaking that pane of glass. While you may occasionally brush the pane of glass with your hand, you want to avoid hitting your head against it and breaking the glass. This will require you to keep your back fairly straight and your gestures close to your body. This will feel unnatural and downright wrong if you've been scolded for using dinosaur arms when presenting live, but as with most new skills, with practice, this will soon come naturally when you are on camera.

But I'm Not a Gesturer!

If you're not much of a gesturer, all of this talk about gestures may have you questioning whether you are at a disadvantage for not using your hands on video. The answer is, yes, but it doesn't have to be all or nothing. Here's why: Because video calls and meetings typically provide much less movement than we are used to in a live environment, no movement can be as repetitive as too much movement on video. Gestures make you more three-dimensional and give your customer more to connect with, beyond just a talking head. Without any gestures, you place a heavy communication load on your face, eyes, voice, and words. And lastly, the ability to see someone's hands contributes to greater trust, as mentioned earlier.

While a non-gesturer need not set their sights on becoming a fervent "hand-talker," sprinkling in a few simple gestures on video calls to emphasize critical points or convey emotion is easy to do and ultimately improves your communication.

PRO TIP:

Regardless of whether you choose to gesture, always make sure that you maintain open body language. For example, avoid crossing your arms, leaning back, or angling yourself away from the camera.

Tips for Standing on Video

Although standing is more common when recording video, it is becoming increasingly popular for live video calls and meetings. Many people find it helps break up a long day of sitting at their desk and they enjoy the extra boost of energy that standing provides. Standing also has the advantage of allowing your customer to see more of your body language and your environment. Here are a few tips specific to standing on video:

1. **Keep the Focus on Your Face.**
   Don't stand so far back that your customer has trouble reading your face and your eyes. Make sure you are framed so that your face and your eyes, particularly, are the focus of attention. This likely means no more than waist-high framing.

2. **Adopt the Right Posture.**
   Proper standing posture on video is back straight, shoulders down and back, arms loose at your sides *(not in your pockets)*, and feet planted no wider than shoulder-width apart.

3. **Distribute Your Weight Equally on Both Feet.**
   Leaning or a slightly uneven stance is more noticeable on video than in person *(and it's pretty noticeable in person!)*.

4. **Avoid the Video Cha-Cha.**
   This is the tricky part. No matter what happens on the upper half of your body, try to keep your lower body still. *(Remember, you are not a duck!)* If you're used to moving around when you present, standing still in one place will seem unnatural at first. However, it looks much more unnatural to your audience when you move in front of the camera. Here's why:

   Stepping toward the camera to connect with your customer or reinforce a point, creates an awkward dance as you realize once you reach the camera, you have nowhere to go except back to where you started! And since you don't want to turn your back to the camera, you are forced to walk backwards to your original spot—which very few people can do gracefully. I've seen people engage in this back and forth, deadly cha-cha for an entire call. *(And while I remember the cha-cha, I remember little else of the call!)*

5. **Channel Movement Energy Into Other Areas.**
   Just like gesturing, don't stifle the energy that inspired you to move. Instead, try channeling that energy into specific gestures, your expression, or your voice. If appropriate, you might use a whiteboard or annotation tool to illustrate your idea.

Two Ways to Improve Your Video Body Language

To become a more effective communicator on video you need to practice, both on and off camera. Practicing on camera by looking at your image when you gesture (only when practicing!) will help you identify whether gestures are in frame, precise, and clear. Practicing off camera in the real world will help you develop the muscle memory that makes these movements become second nature on video.

For example, standing still in front of the camera with all of the action taking place in your upper body, your head, and your arms requires quite a bit of practice and focus. The last thing you want to do when you're on an important video call is fight the urge to move. So you start by practicing on video on your own and add in some off-video practice, like standing still while waiting in line at the grocery store or when you're on a phone call. That way your new behavior won't feel so foreign when you step in front of the camera for an actual call or meeting.

One gesture I struggled to master on video was holding up my fingers when referring to different points. Although I felt like I was holding my hands up where they could be seen by my audience, upon review, my fingers floated along at the bottom of the screen before quickly disappearing altogether. My attempt at gesturing not only didn't support what I was saying, but it also added an unnecessary distraction.

Initially, I practiced on camera. I identified the sweet spot of just where my hands and fingers needed to be positioned and how long I needed to leave them up to remain visible on screen *(I recommend at least five seconds)*. Then, I started practicing off camera in everyday life. For example, whenever I would share a specific number of steps or points, I would raise my arm and gesture with the corresponding number of fingers. Thanks to the on and off camera combo, I was soon able to naturally hit the mark on video without thinking about it.

A word of caution: I was at dinner numerating the steps involved in an upcoming project to my husband a few months later. Before I could get to step two, my husband put his fork down and said gently, “You really don’t have to count things out for me anymore.” Point taken! Just like not all in-person gestures work on video, not all video gestures work face-to-face. In a hybrid selling world, you, like me, will need to be able to speak both languages fluently.

A Last Note About Authenticity

Some people are gesturers, some aren’t. Some people are prone to move, others are content to stay still. While I don’t want you to turn into someone you’re not, I’ve found that many people hold themselves back from gesturing, which means they’re holding back their personality and the opportunity for people to get to know them. Notice how you move and gesture when you’re telling a story or talking to good friends. That is the level of animation that you want to achieve and adapt for the screen. If you’re falling short of that on video, you’re capable of greater expression than you’re allowing your audience to see.

EXERCISE
DEVELOP VIDEO-FRIENDLY BODY LANGUAGE

The first step to better body language on video is to observe how you are currently using movement and gestures. Record yourself in a typical presentation or meeting. Review your recording focusing exclusively on your body language. Then ask yourself the following:

Are your movements within your frame, or is there too much activity taking place out of frame?

Are your gestures specific and clear?

Do your gestures support what you're saying, or do they distract from it?

Are you in a gesture rut? (i.e., repeatedly using the same gesture for a wide variety of thoughts.)

Are there places where your message could benefit from a specific gesture?

Make notes on what you need to finetune. Schedule a practice session in front of your camera where you repeatedly try to hit the mark on each gesture. Take it offline and practice those same gestures in your daily life. Soon, you'll be naturally and effortlessly incorporating gestures and movements that enhance or expand your audience's understanding.

CHAPTER 9

USING EXPRESSION TO SUPER-CHARGE YOUR RELATIONSHIPS

If your face has nothing to say, why have your camera on?

JULIE HANSEN

Why are emails so often misinterpreted? Why do we use emoticons in texts? Because on their own, words are insufficient at communicating emotion. Facial expressions are your emoticons on video. If you're not using them you may not be clearly communicating empathy and interest—two key ingredients necessary for relationships to grow. And you are also denying your customer the opportunity to really get to know you.

To build a meaningful relationship with another person, you have to be vulnerable. And part of that vulnerability is letting your customer see how you feel about what you're saying or hearing. When your face doesn't communicate any emotion, you are like that detached newscaster who delivers devastating or fantastic news with the same neutral expression. On the other hand, when your face conveys an inappropriate expression, you create confusion and damage your credibility.

In this chapter you'll learn what your face is communicating to your audience and how to make sure that it aligns with your intention. You'll also discover how to express yourself in an authentic way that supports your message and makes your customer feel understood.

Emotions and Business: An Uneasy Partnership

Many people are uncomfortable expressing feelings freely in business. Early on in our careers we learn to put the brakes on our emotions, and thus our expressions, for fear of appearing unprofessional or not serious. In person, you might get away with this business poker face because it's offset by your energy or your overall body language. But on video, your face looms disproportionately large. To not use your face to enhance communication and build relationships is a poor use of prime real estate. Yet jump on any video call today and you will see a swath of blank faces, from the presenter to the audience. It begs the question: if your face has nothing to say, why have your camera on?

Consider the case of Jeff; a young business development rep sent to me by his sales manager:

"Technically, Jeff is doing everything right," Jeff's manager explained. "I can't put my finger on why he is struggling to get prospects to take the next step and commit to a product demo."

After watching a recording of Jeff with a prospect, it was clear to me what was missing. Although Jeff said all the right words, asked the right questions, established need and value, his face was a textbook example of Resting Business Face. From *hello* to *goodbye*, his expression remained unrelentingly neutral. When the prospect brought up a rather significant problem she was experiencing with her current solution, not a glimmer of empathy or understanding crossed Jeff's face. When Jeff shared that a recent prospect had saved nearly $100,000 a year by solving this problem with Jeff's company's product, his face bore the same expression that one might use to say, "pass the salt."

It's not just customers who show up on calls with Resting Business Face. Sellers are equally guilty of reflecting that same blank video face back to their customers, and it's as frustrating and unfulfilling for them as it is for you. RBF is the facial equivalent of the monotone voice, and it severely limits your ability to form a relationship with your customer or make an impact with your words. If you are not using your face to communicate, the only thing you've proven to your customer is that you are not a bot.

Emotions Worth Expressing in Business

Human beings were nonlanguage creatures for hundreds of thousands of years. Barring a few grunts here and there, we learned to communicate through body language and facial expression. Just like back in the cave days, our face can quickly convey numerous feelings, thoughts, and intentions, from empathy to passion to understanding. While your customer may not be a trained lip reader, they are, like you, an experienced face reader, so it's important to know *just what is your face saying?*

There are myriad emotions you may want to communicate with your customer to further your relationship. While love and hate are a bit dramatic for a business meeting, there are plenty of feelings that may be very appropriate and desirable to share with your customer, including:

- Joy
- Gratitude
- Enthusiasm
- Surprise
- Empathy
- Shock
- Displeasure
- Concern
- Doubt

Not every statement that comes out of your mouth calls for a matching expression. As with body language, you don't want to overdo and fall into melodrama! But a few authentic expressions can underscore key points, validate your customers' feelings, thoughts, and ideas, and encourage your customer to open up and express themselves as well.

Why Being Expressive on Video Is Easier Said Than Done

Knowing that you need to be more expressive on video doesn't always make it happen. Well-worn behaviors and the unique challenges of communicating on video may be inhibiting you from using your expressive powers to your fullest. Some of the factors that may be working against your attempts to express yourself on video include:

- **Receiving Mode.** You too, have been conditioned to settle in as a passive observer when you sit in front of a screen. Your words may be working hard, but your face may be stuck in RBF by force of habit.
- **Tension.** Video calls with customers and prospects aren't like calls with your friends, family, or parent teacher group. There is much more at stake and plenty of moving parts to monitor, so it's common to feel some nerves. This stress often leads to tension which can cause your facial muscles to tighten up as well, making it difficult to express yourself freely, both vocally and physically.
- **Energy depletion.** It takes energy to smile and emote! Much of that energy that gives you a sparkle in person disappears on video simply because you are two-dimensional and are communicating through a screen.
- **Disconnect between feelings and face.** For many people, what they are feeling is not automatically expressed on their face. That smile you think you're sharing may not even be registering on your face at all to your audience.

These are all factors that can be overcome with self-awareness, practice, and an understanding of how the camera reads expressions. But all of this is moot unless we strive for absolute authenticity.

Start from a Place of Authenticity.

I was on a call with a sales rep whose service I was interested in, so much so that I was only slightly suspicious of the forced smile he wore for most of our conversation. At the end of the meeting my suspicions were confirmed when his smile was quickly replaced with a scowl after he thought he had exited the meeting.

Many salespeople have been told to paste on a phony smile before talking to a customer. Smile and dial, right? That may work on the phone, but remember, the camera is a lie detector. Fake emotions are easy to spot on video and may do more harm than good. While forcing yourself to smile does have the potential to induce a positive mood, don't convince yourself that it will fool your virtual audience for long. A genuine smile uses more muscles than a fake one, including those involuntary muscles around your mouth, cheeks, forehead, and eyes. A forced or polite smile uses only the outer muscles around your mouth.[xxxix] Of course, your customer won't be aware of which muscles you're engaging, but they will intuitively know that something is off, casting doubt on your sincerity.

Try this for yourself. Get in front of a mirror. Now, think of an incident or a person that makes you smile. Maybe it's a funny meme, a loved one's sweet comment or action, or an adorable child or pet. Notice your smile in the mirror. That is a genuine smile. Now think of something that makes you unhappy *(People never seem to need suggestions in this area!)*. Ponder this negative thought for a minute, then quickly force yourself to smile. Recheck the mirror. Notice the difference? Now, ask yourself honestly: would you trust that person with the phony smile staring back at you?

Authentic expression comes from a feeling or an emotion. If your muscles are warm and you're a naturally expressive person, simply getting in touch with that feeling often is enough to light up your face with the proper expression. That's why it's important to be clear about how you feel about a subject and to allow yourself to feel as strongly as possible about it.

If you're indifferent about a particular topic or too detached from it, you may struggle to find that organic expressiveness. This frequently happens on video. It's easy to detach from feelings and go on autopilot when rushing from one video call to the next. But as mentioned in Chapter 2, you must take a moment to stop and think about why you're talking to each specific person. What problem are you solving for them? What happens if they don't solve the problem or choose the wrong solution? Tapping into why your conversation really matters can quickly trigger these emotions.

Once you've connected to a strong reason to communicate and warmed up your expressive muscles, your face will take it from there—most of the time.

Reconnect Your Face to Your Feelings.

Despite feeling deeply about your customer's situation and your role in helping them transcend it, you may find that those feelings are not being displayed on your face. Much like my surprise when the director showed me what my face looked like during rehearsal, and it was nothing like what I was feeling. Apparently the signal that I was happy had failed to travel from my brain to my face!

Most people have a default expression that they remain largely unaware of. If your default is smiling, congratulations! You have a head start. If your default is RBF like me, you and I have some work to do. Like many business professionals, those years of repressing your instincts may have—pardon my highly simplified description here—disconnected the wiring between your face and your feelings. What can you do when you feel empathy, happiness, concern, or hope, but your face isn't communicating those emotions? You can learn to use your facial muscles more consciously and re-train those atrophied expressive muscles with the warm-up exercises at the end of this chapter.

Your Smile: a Virtual Superpower

I may not know you, but I know that you need to smile more on video.

No, I haven't been stalking you. But I have been on thousands of video calls and meetings and observed that smiles are as rare as a signed contract on a cold call. And when a seller does smile, it's like a shooting star—don't blink or you'll miss it! It's not just a welcome change to see people smile on video, it's a powerful expression that your audience associates with friendliness, approachability, and compassion. All are important traits for building a solid relationship.

While a smile is certainly inappropriate when discussing a customer's pain points or a price increase, a video message or presentation delivered by the grim reaper can quickly wear on your audience. Surely you can find the occasional reason to smile in your conversation! Are you sharing a benefit? Smile. Are you solving a problem? Smile. Let your customer know that you have good news. Is your customer sharing a personal or professional success with you? Smile. Let them know that you're happy for them or that you're enjoying the conversation.

Half-Smiles Don't Count.

Here's the funny thing about smiling *(pun intended)*, half-smiles don't cut it. Lisa Gherardini, the real-life model for Da Vinci's famous Mona Lisa painting, may not have succeeded on video. That slight upturn at the corners of her mouth would have been nearly imperceptible to a virtual audience. You must fully commit to smiling or the camera (and therefore, your customer) may not register it as a smile.

How do you know when you have a video-friendly smile on your face? Of course, you can review one of your recordings and see for yourself, but there's an easier and more practical way to know if you are smiling sufficiently enough for your audience to see it.

Have you ever laughed so hard your cheeks hurt? Why do they hurt? Because an ear-to-ear smile involves more muscles than a half-smile. When you're smiling fully, you should be able to feel the muscles in your cheeks move, not just the corners of your mouth. Unlike half-smiles, full smiles also require your lips to be parted. That means with a full smile you can feel the air on your teeth when you breathe in. Next time you think you're smiling, make sure you feel those signals. You don't want to be the Mona Lisa of video.

Master the Art of Smeaking
(Smiling + Speaking)

I spent a few years in Toastmasters finetuning my keynotes, and there was one woman in our group who always held my attention. She wasn't the best technical speaker, and her subject wasn't always relevant to me, yet she drew me in week after week. One day I realized her secret. She had mastered the art of smiling plus speaking, or smeaking.

Smeaking is not only engaging, but it's also contagious.[xi] While watching this woman speak, I felt the corners of my mouth turn up in response. Glancing around the room, it was clear others were equally affected.

If you are like my Toastmaster friend and smiling while speaking is already in your wheelhouse, you are fortunate indeed! If you're more like me, you will need to practice. Start by finding places to smile on video. Greeting your customer is a perfect place for a smile. After you say "hello," resist the urge to release that smile. Try holding onto your smile until you have another emotion or thought come along to take its place. Soon you'll be smeaking without thinking about it!

EXERCISES
WARMING-UP YOUR EXPRESSIVE MUSCLES

1. **Big Face – Little Face**
   Find a private space. *(Trust me, you don't want anyone you care about to see this!)* Open your mouth, your eyes, and your nostrils as wide as you can. And then, open them even farther! Hold this position for ten to twenty seconds. Then right away, tighten your entire face. Scrunch it up as much as possible. Like one of those shrunken apple faces that you made as a kid. Hold this for ten to twenty seconds. Repeat this whole process five or six times and your face will be energized and loose.

2. **Go Over-the-Top (Expression Version)**
   You were introduced to this exercise in Chapter 3 to energize your body; but it's also extremely effective for activating the expressive muscles in your face. Take your presentation, your pitch, or any type of content, and read it out loud with all the enthusiasm and energy you can possibly muster. *(If you don't have to close your doors or windows, you're not going big enough.)* Focus on using as many facial muscles as possible to express each idea. Over-dramatize any emotional or descriptive words. This will not only warm up your facial expressions but also your voice.

CHAPTER 10

BRINGING YOUR MESSAGE TO LIFE WITH YOUR VOICE

Video killed the radio star.

THE BUGGLES, BAND

The Buggles were wrong. Video did not, as predicted, “kill the radio star” or lower the importance of the voice when it comes to engaging, influencing, and connecting with others. The sound, quality, and tone of your voice can bring your message to life on video... or cause it to fade into oblivion. Many vocal challenges that are easily overlooked when face-to-face are magnified on video, making it easy for your customer to tune you out, misinterpret your meaning, or form an inaccurate impression of you.

For example:

- Sara’s natural enthusiasm on video calls is impressive, as is her ability to speak rapidly and at length without oxygen. Unfortunately, this steady stream of words wears down her audience and makes it impossible to pull out the key points hidden within.
- Like a song played entirely on the note of C, Ahmad delivers every word of his presentation at the same level, causing even eager audience members to drift off. His message is strong—but if no one’s listening, does it matter?
- Hayley, a senior salesperson with a soft voice and a tendency to end most sentences on an uptick, complains of being frequently interrupted or talked over in virtual meetings. She suspects that had something to do with recently being passed over for a managerial position.

None of these problems are related to content or messaging. They are vocal issues that can seriously impact your relationship and career goals. Misusing your voice can be as detrimental as delivering the wrong sales message or forgetting to ask for the business.

Many factors contribute to the way your voice sounds on video and whether you are drawing your audience in or shutting them out.

The Importance of Vocal Clarity on Video

Perhaps you've been on a video call where the speaker was difficult to hear, either because they spoke too fast or the sound quality was poor. Did you address the issue with them? Or, like many people, did you tolerate it for a while, only to eventually give up and find your attention wandering? While others will be quick to tell you, "you're on mute" or "you're breaking up," they're not likely to tell you your voice is flat and passionless, or you sound like you're calling from inside a closet.

One of the first objectives on video (or in person) is to make it as easy as possible for your audience to hear you and understand you. The quality should be as if you are sitting across from each other in a quiet spot. That means your customer shouldn't have to strain to hear you, nor should you have to strain to communicate. If you are using your voice correctly and have proper equipment, you shouldn't have to push your voice at all.

Of course, a good microphone is vital, and you may want to review Chapter 4 to make sure you are at the correct distance from your microphone. But the most expensive microphone in the world can't make a flat voice engaging, eliminate filler words, or slow you down to a tolerable pace. Most microphones simply magnify bad vocal habits.

The Difference Between Vocal Energy and Volume

People rarely speak with as much personality or energy on video as they do when visiting with others face-to-face. This is dangerous because low energy often makes people sound uninterested or indifferent. It takes a high level of energy to keep a customer engaged with your voice; however, many people make the mistake of assuming that more energy means speaking louder.

Joel Goldberg, pre-and post-game host for the Kansas City Royals, puts it this way, "It is different on camera. There's this fine line as a broadcaster and as an actor between energy and volume. I think that until we figure it out, we think when someone says, 'have more energy,' they mean you need to get louder."

Most people don't need to add volume to their voice. They need to add energy. As a stage actor, I learned to project to the back row of the theater. This did not prepare me for my first television commercial shoot. When the director asked me to do another take with "more energy," I practically shouted my lines at the camera. By the pained expression on the director's face, it was apparent this was not what he had in mind.

Unlike in person, on video you are much closer to your audience. Your customer will typically be seated the face-to-face equivalent of fewer than two feet from you. Raising your volume at this distance may feel to your customer like you are shouting at them. Instead, try raising your energy. Then channel that energy into bringing your words to life with body language (as in the previous chapter), or with your voice by adding color, tone, and variety using the exercises at the end of this chapter.

Pace Yourself.

How fast or slow you speak plays an important role in your customer's attention and understanding. Speak too quickly, and they may become frustrated, lose track, miss your point, and eventually tune out. Talk too slowly, and you try your customer's patience, making them prey to distractions *(or pray for distractions!)*.

Most sellers talk too fast on video calls. Even sellers who speak at an easy-to-follow pace in person rush unnecessarily on video calls. This typically happens for one of three reasons:

1. Sellers are unable to see their customer's body language. They conclude (often falsely) that those reactions are negative and start to speed up and eliminate crucial pauses.

2. Sellers can see their customer, but the expression or body language of their customer seems to indicate they are bored or disinterested. The seller takes this evidence as proof and it's off to the races!

3. Sellers are nervous or excited because the stakes are high, they're speaking to a large group, or they're uncertain of their content, messaging, or technology.

The first two issues—an inability to see their customer or being rattled by what they see—can be easily addressed by using the Act As If method outlined in Chapter 6. Envisioning the customer gazing back at you with interest, perhaps nodding at your key points, is often enough to get you to pause occasionally and achieve a more conversational pace.

The third issue, speeding up when you're nervous or excited, is very common. Doing some relaxation and breathing exercises prior to your call or recording will help. You can also channel that excess energy into communicating your message as clearly as possible by slowing down and articulating your words rather than letting your words run away with you. Some people find that imagining they are speaking to an audience for whom English is a second language helpful in slowing down their pace.

What if your customer *is* bored? Even if you confirm that your customer is uninterested, distracted, or in a hurry, racing through your presentation or talking points is never the solution to a negative reaction. Instead, find out what is of interest to them and then cut to the chase. Shift your focus to that most crucial section.

> PRO TIP
>
> **If your presentation or pitch is organized into chunks, you can jump around on the fly, but never rush. Rushing devalues your message and conveys a lack of confidence. Taking your time on a few key areas is much more effective than racing through a dozen points that your customer will never remember.**

The All-Important (and Difficult) Virtual Pause

Video calls have essentially become a punctuation-free zone. It's commonplace for salespeople and presenters to share one thought, proceeded by another, and another. Each thought is loosely strung together with an occasional comma or transition word, like *so*, *and*, *but*, *while*, or *then*.

This is often a defensive reaction to an unusually passive audience. Customers are much less likely to interact or to jump in during those pauses than they were in person. While it is uncomfortable to pause after asking a question or delivering a message, a relationship is built on a dialogue, not a monologue. By not taking the time to pause you put the responsibility solely on your customer to interrupt you. Rather than do that, most people shut down completely.

An effective technique is to think about speaking with punctuation. Surprisingly, punctuation isn't just for written content. Its purpose is to clarify your message to the receiver, ensure comprehension, and allow for feedback. And as we learned earlier, message misinterpretation and lack of feedback are two of the most common areas where the communication loop breaks down on video.

How to Create a More Natural Conversation with Punctuation

We tend to naturally and subconsciously use punctuation when speaking to someone face-to-face. We end questions with a question mark. We slow down after a comma or stop at a period. On video we have to be more conscious of applying punctuation in order to improve clarity and allow space for our customers to participate in the conversation. Below are a few ways to use vocal punctuation:

- **Vocal periods.** When you finish a thought, sentence, or a point you want your audience to remember (like a competitive differentiator or value proposition), visualize a period at the end of it and pause for a few seconds. This hard stop at the end of a sentence allows the impact of your words to stick before you move on to the next thought or point. A vocal period also gives your customer an opportunity to respond, or at least to digest what's been said. Rushing through this space interrupts that vital process for your customer. *(Bonus: If you stop long enough, your prospect may actually tell you something that you wouldn't have found out if you'd kept talking!)*
- **Vocal commas.** If you're delivering a clearly defined list of options, ideas, or points, make it easier for your customer to retain them by taking a short pause between each point and changing the tone of your voice to differentiate one from the other.
- **Vocal question marks.** Too many questions on video go unanswered simply because they don't sound like questions. Interrogative words, like who, what, where, when, and why are often not enough to alert your audience that a question has been posed. If you tack a question onto the end of a long, run-on sentence and deliver it in the same flat tone, it's easy for your audience to miss it entirely.

  To improve your response rate, precede each question with a pause so that a clear separation exists between telling and asking. Visualize a question mark at the end of your sentence. This gives your tone the needed uptick to let your audience know that you expect an answer.

There's no need to race through your video calls. By picturing an engaged person or adding vocal punctuation you will speak at a more natural pace, and your customer will be more attentive and responsive.

Add Variety with Your Vocal Tools.

Your voice is capable of playing a symphony, yet on video, most salespeople settle for "Chopsticks." If you deliver every word at the same pace, tone, or level, it will wear on your audience like a steadily dripping faucet. There's a reason why we're more likely to fall asleep listening to a repetitive pattern, such as white noise. Variety in your speech is not just more pleasant to listen to, it's necessary to maintain audience attention—especially in a virtual environment.[xli]

Like your face, your voice should tell your customer how you feel about what you're saying. Good news should sound different than bad news, and important points different than non-essential.

To achieve variety in your voice, you can access your many vocal tools. In addition to speaking with punctuation, your vocal tools include **volume**, **tone**, **emphasis**, **range**, **pace**, and of course, **the pause**. Volume, while effective in person, is probably where you will use the least variety on video. The other tools can all be used in moderation. For example, you could speed up or use a vocal exclamation point when sharing something exciting. You could emphasize keywords when you are reinforcing a point. You might change your tone when asking a question or switching to a new topic. Increasing the number of notes you play, and when you play them, goes a long way toward keeping virtual audiences attentive and engaged.

Warm-up Your Voice.

Most people think that their voice is warm because they've been talking, but that is not necessarily the case. You may not be using your vocal cords, your mouth, and your breath to showcase your voice at its best. In fact, you may be hurting your voice by straining, or you may be stuck in a monotone delivery or speaking too softly or breathlessly. By investing a little time warming up each part of your mouth and playing with your vocal tools, your true voice will start to emerge, and you'll have greater success holding your audience's attention.

EXERCISE

AMP UP YOUR VOCAL VARIETY

Speaking in that monotone business voice is a habit, and like any habit, it's often necessary to shake things up to break out of it. The exercises below will help you add more variety in your voice:

- **Run scales.** Think of your voice as floating on a scale. Start by taking a deep breath. On an exhale make a long vowel sound (like "eeh") starting at the highest note on your scale, then try to smoothly slide down the scale to the lowest point as you complete your exhale. Reverse and start at your lowest point and slide up the scale.
- **Mix it up.** If you're a fast talker, you don't need to turn into a slow talker and vice versa. But try alternating a quicker pace with a slower pace to mix things up for your customer and allow them a chance to catch up.
- **Read Dr. Seuss.** Reading children's books out loud in as animated a voice as possible is a fun and easy way to warm up and add a variety of colors and shades to your voice.

CHAPTER 11

MANAGING ATTENTION AND CREATING INTERACTION IN VIRTUAL MEETINGS

The play was a great success, but the audience was a disaster.

OSCAR WILDE, PLAYWRIGHT

After DeWayne's virtual sales presentation fell flat, he complained to me about how unresponsive his audience was.

"I told them upfront that I wanted this to be more of a conversation, but they didn't give me anything to work with. No questions, nothing. I gave that same presentation to a similar group in person, and there were tons of questions and it turned into a great discussion." DeWayne shrugged, "I don't get it."

Attention and interaction are critical to create and grow a relationship or drive sales.[xlii] Yet most virtual calls, presentations, and demos end up as painful monologues, often because sellers duplicate what was successful face-to-face. Unfortunately, many of the things that worked beautifully to facilitate interaction live don't produce the same results on video. For example, over video, you can't encourage someone to answer a question or volunteer to share by singling them out with a steady, directed gaze or moving physically closer to them.

And unlike in a live meeting, most participants feel little or no obligation to at least feign attention. In a virtual world, people feel free to browse their computer screen, check their phone, or enjoy a hearty meal while on a call.

Although it's easy to blame poor engagement on your audience, it's not their responsibility to interact with you. Customers are just doing what they have been trained to do when sitting in front of a screen: passively observe. Double down on that if they're expecting you to deliver a presentation or demonstration. While you might occasionally encounter a more actively engaged audience, virtual interaction rarely just happens on its own. As the salesperson, it is your responsibility to create both the desire and the opportunity for customers to interact with you.

Too many people think of interaction as lobbing a few questions at their audience or inviting them to type something into chat. With audience attention spans spinning ever downward and the variety of distractions multiplying, random acts of engagement rarely work.[xliii] To achieve the level of interaction necessary to turn a passive viewer into an active participant on video, you need to have a plan. And this plan should take into account what drives virtual attention and social behaviors online, and how to use all available interaction tools.

Four Key Factors to Drive Attention on Video

There are four key factors to consider when it comes to gaining and maintaining audience attention on video: movement, relevancy, variety, and attention span limitations.

1. **Movement**

   As you've seen in earlier chapters, movement is a highly effective way to get someone's attention on video. Movement can be through your body language, gestures, or expressions, or it can be an activity taking place on your customer's screen (e.g., animations, transitions, annotations, etc.). Since your customer will be as drawn to unintended movement as much as planned or purposeful movement, it's vital that you control any unnecessary activity on your screen.

2. **Relevancy**

   Any type of engagement or interaction should always be relevant and purposeful. Blatant or unconnected attention-grabbers that lead nowhere waste time and try the patience of busy customers.

While silly backgrounds or pointless videos may be fine for calls with friends and family, a business call or meeting is a deliberate, heightened communication. Therefore, most elements, including engagement, should be tied to the reason that you are there.

3. **Variety**

   Humans adapt to patterns.[xliv] Many presentations are an endless parade of slides or rely too heavily on a single form of engagement, such as repeatedly asking, "does that make sense?" Customers quickly adapt to these patterns, reducing the power of that tool to keep them engaged.

4. **Attention Span Limitations**

   It's a losing battle to talk to people who are physically or mentally unable to pay attention. Just like people require biological breaks, your prospect needs an attention break to reset as well. Ignoring the limitations of your audience's ability to focus is a common (and costly) mistake in virtual communications.

   There are two general time markers to consider as you plan your video call or meeting. The first consideration is overall meeting length. Most people are accustomed to face-to-face meetings breaking after fifty or sixty minutes. This length of time is ingrained in us from our earliest school days and it's currently built into most calendars. Many people schedule virtual meetings back-to-back on the hour, so fifty minutes is about as long as you should go. Any longer and you are at risk of losing your audience or causing a resentment.

   The second time marker is how long your audience can stay focused on a single idea or topic. Most presentations are structured around how long it takes to present a particular topic, not the length of the audience's attention span. This results in a lot of great points falling flat simple because the presenter didn't account for the predictable ebb and flow of attention.

Studies show that attention naturally wanes after two to five minutes (the length of a song is a good example) and continues to drop if left unchecked.[xiv] In order to combat this decline, try organizing your content into two-to-five-minute snack-sized chunks. Often times a simple change of topic or focus between those chunks will be sufficient to refresh attention, but it's also a good idea to work in some form of interaction or a change in speakers.

Twelve Ways to Improve Virtual Interaction

Having an attentive customer is a start, but most successful sales calls include a high level of interaction between the seller and the buyer. In fact, in their analysis of 67,149 sales demos, Gong.io didn't find a single closed deal when the seller spoke for more than seventy-six seconds uninterrupted. Based on that, I bet many of us have some room for improvement in this area! Below are some tactics that will help make greater interaction possible on video:

1. **Interact Early.**

   If you give a ten-minute monologue before interacting with your audience, expect to hear nothing but crickets when you do try to engage them. During those crucial first few minutes of any meeting or call, you train your audience on what their role is and how you expect them to participate in the meeting. In most cases, your business audience will arrive at a virtual meeting fully prepared to settle into their role as passive observers. If you don't shake this up early and realign expectations, you will find it difficult to engage customers later in the meeting.

2. **Start with a Slam Dunk.**

   Ask an easy question in those first few minutes of your meeting. One that requires a *yes* or a *no* response or a choice between A and B. Your goal is not necessarily to learn from the answer but to get your audience used to interacting, so make it easy. If you have multiple people on the call, ask them to type in a simple response in chat or raise their hands. Getting your audience in the habit of interacting early will increase their responsiveness as you move on to questions requiring greater introspection.

3. **Drop the Wishful Thinking.**

   Perhaps, like DeWayne, you assume that asking your audience upfront to "please ask questions as you go" or saying, "let's make this interactive" is sufficient. While certainly reasonable requests, be prepared for them to fall on deaf ears. This is white noise to customers by now. You must take more direct action to make interaction feel like a requirement, not an option.

4. **Ask Simple Questions.**

   I don't mean that all your questions have to be softballs. Thought-provoking questions are OK as long as you're prepared to wait a little longer for the answer. By simple, I mean easy for your customer to remember and formulate a response to without needing to have the question repeated.

   Many well-intentioned questions are met with a resounding silence because they require too much work on the part of the participant! This includes questions that are longer than twenty seconds or questions that contain multiple parts. Both turn into unwelcome memory tests. Often, when you ask a multi-part question your audience won't respond at all unless they know the answer to all question parts. To improve the likelihood of receiving a response, simply break multi-part questions into several individual questions and ask them one at a time. It's also helpful to use question trigger words (*who, what, where, when, why,* or *how*) to alert your customer that there is a question ahead.

5. **Expect an Answer.**

   Another reason your questions may not elicit a response is that the customer is not convinced that you really expect a verbal answer from them. When you are not fully committed to receiving an answer to your question, your voice will lack the right tenor and necessary uptick to indicate you expect a response. This lack of clarity introduces just enough doubt to allow your customer to feel comfortable not answering. Adding a verbal question mark (as suggested in the previous chapter) may help, but you also must make the decision internally that you do indeed expect an answer to your question. Even if it's just, "I don't know." By approaching each question with complete determination to receive an answer, your voice will find the right intonation and your face the necessary expression to convince your customer that silence is not an option.

6. **Look at the Camera.**
   If you were standing across from your customer, would you ask them a question while staring at their shoes? That's the virtual equivalent of asking a question while looking at your screen and not the camera. While one might expect this evasive eye contact from a middle schooler asking his crush to the school dance, it's completely unacceptable and unsuccessful in business, whether in person or on video.

   To ensure that your customer knows that you expect a response to your question, consistently deliver it while focused on the camera, not your customer's image on your screen.

   When you have a larger audience or team at your meeting, it's even more crucial that you look at the camera when asking a question. Without this visual cue, it's easy for everyone on the call to defer responsibility and assume that someone else will answer it. Looking at the camera makes each person feel like you are speaking just to them, thus increasing your likelihood of a response.

7. **Embrace the Pause.**
   Letting a question hang in silence for more than a few seconds is even more nerve-racking on video than in person because you can't see your customer processing your question or considering their response. But remain strong! If you jump in to answer your

own question, your customer will happily let you handle the remainder of your questions as well. In the process, you are short-circuiting a very important internal process that takes place for each member of your audience.

What Happens When You Ask a Question on a Video Call?

When you pose a question to a group of two or more people, the silence that follows is not the dead air you imagine it to be. There is a lot taking place, as you'll see in the example below:

SALESPERSON:

"What types of challenges are you seeing in this particular area?"

AUDIENCE MEMBER:

0-3 Seconds: Processing *(What challenges am I seeing?)*

3-6 Seconds: Formulating *(It certainly takes me a lot of time to pull data for weekly reports.)*

6-9 Seconds: Debating *(Should I share it? Or will my manager think I'm just slow?)*

9-12 Seconds: Negotiating *(Bob has a lot to say. I'm sure he will answer this.)*

12-15 Seconds: Pressure *(I guess Bob's not going to take this. Maybe I should jump in.)*

15-17 Seconds: Unmuting self

17+ Seconds: Answer! "One of the things I've seen in my department is..."

While you don't necessarily need to wait a full seventeen seconds after posing every question, you can see the need to leave sufficient space for your audience to grapple with this process. I recommend waiting in silence for at least ten seconds, and even then, don't answer the question for your audience. Instead, invite someone to answer by using their name, or prompt your audience with an example of how others like them have responded to your question. If, for instance, after asking the above question you are met with fifteen seconds of silence, you might say, "One of the things we hear from our other customers is that they're spending an awful lot of time pulling data together for reports. Is that something you're experiencing as well?"

Do this a few times and your audience will soon understand that you expect them to participate.

8. Name First, Then Question

Were you ever caught daydreaming in school, snapping to attention only after hearing the teacher call your name? I was, and it wasn't a good feeling. Yet that's often what we do to our customers when we pose a question and tack their name onto the end of it. Save them the painful flashback or embarrassment in front of their peers by giving your customer a clear signal when you have a question coming their way.

For example: "Hey Jonathan, I know that your team uses a lot of Excel spreadsheets to pull those reports together. How much time would you say your team spends on that during an average week?"

This courtesy has even more importance with large groups, as most people feel justified to remain silent in a crowd.

9. Interact More Frequently.

You want to get your audience interacting early and often. If you have organized your presentation or meeting into two-to-five-minute snack-sized chunks, as mentioned earlier, the end of a chunk can serve as a helpful cue to introduce some form of interaction, e.g., ask a question, launch a poll, show a video, etc.

10. Use Your Platform Tools.

Most video conferencing platforms are equipped with chat, polls, reactions, whiteboards, annotations, and even breakout rooms. Be quite clear about which tools you want your audience to use. Don't overwhelm them with too many choices. Some people may be unfamiliar with the platform, so deliver instructions slowly and precisely. You may need to repeat those instructions several times for a larger group or display them clearly on a slide. Once you have given them instructions, give your audience a few more seconds to respond than feels comfortable.

11. Summarize Often.

Summarizing is essential in face-to-face meetings and presentations, but they take on a greater significance on video as listeners can dip in and out of the meeting at will. In addition, summarizing key points often brings to the surface questions that may have occurred to your audience but not been fully formed while you were speaking.

12. Rephrase your Questions.

You may have picked up on my low opinion of the overused and potentially condescending check-in question, "Does that make sense?" So what types of questions will encourage your audience to break their code of silence on video? Often times a more specific question, like, "What is the average length of your sales cycle?" produces results. Unique questions, like "What would your ideal review say about you?" or more encompassing questions, like "Any questions, comments, or observations?" can also be effective. Mixing up the types of questions used also aids in attention and response.

Your Virtual Engagement Tools

It's critical that you have a variety of ways to keep your prospect on their toes in a virtual world. Fortunately, you have many engagement tools in your virtual tool kit to keep attention high.

Annotate Your Screen.

I know I am not alone in finding videos of people drawing, painting, or cooking online oddly compelling. Science has an answer for this: When we watch another person engage in an activity, like drawing, the mirror neurons in our brain fire as if we are the ones participating in the actual activity ourselves.[xlvi] You can fire those mirror neurons in your customer's brain as well by the simple act of writing directly on your slides or screen. Again, be selective about when you use it. Annotating everything will backfire and make your content look more complicated than it is. This feature is available on most platforms and also in PowerPoint.

Animate Your Slides.

Whether it's bullet points appearing and disappearing or images coming and going, occasional movement on your slides will help to draw attention to what you're doing. When using special effects on your slides, keep in mind that a little goes along way because the space is so small. You don't want your audience reaching for their Dramamine or experiencing a lag from too many animations or fancy transitions.

Use Your Mouse or a Laser Pointer.

These tools are designed to draw your audience's attention to a specific focal point, yet few people use them precisely enough on screen to serve that purpose. Instead, they zip around on screen as if they were tormenting a cat with a laser dot!

To avoid this, find the spot you want to highlight on your screen, then point at it. Hold it steady for at least a count of five. Your audience doesn't know where you're headed, so give them a chance to orient themselves to your current position before zipping off to destinations unknown. Also, it's a good idea to provide verbal cues to your audience as well, like, "Now in the upper right corner of your screen you can see the blue tab..." This picks up those members of your audience who may have checked out momentarily or lost track of your mouse, eliminating any confusion.

Go Full Screen.

Don't stay in screen share throughout your entire presentation or pitch. It's difficult enough to stay alert during a live presentation, and that challenge is only more significant in a virtual environment. Leverage the attention-grabbing and relationship-building power of the human face by interspersing screen-sharing with a full screen view of your face. This is an effective way to re-engage and re-connect with your audience throughout your presentation, especially during introductions, summaries, and Q&A.

Leverage Your Voice.

Your voice has the power to snap people back to attention or lull them to sleep. If you're using your voice to simply recite what's on the slide, you are missing the point. Your voice can add context to what you're sharing and convey meaning and emotion. Ensuring that you're in great vocal form should be part of your standard daily preparation.

Paint Word Pictures.

In a virtual presentation, your words have to work even harder than in a live presentation. Think about painting pictures with your words. For example, when describing a benefit, avoid broad generalities. Instead of saying your feature saves your customer money, use specific metrics or examples, such as, "a customer very similar to you was able to save enough money to hire two full-time employees, which freed up his weekends for the first time in ten years."

Choose words that incite emotion or interest. Make your descriptions vivid. Don't overdo the adjectives, focus on highlighting just those points that you want to stand out in your prospect's mind. Listen to your favorite podcasts and radio shows, and notice how professional speakers use descriptive words to keep you engaged.

Tell a Story, Metaphor, or Analogy.

Most business meetings focus on facts and logic. While necessary, facts often ignore the emotional component that engages more areas of the listeners' brain. Breaking your presentation or meeting up with a short, compelling, purposeful story, metaphor or analogy is an effective and memorable way to drive attention.[xlvii] For example, instead of telling your customer they will end up paying a lot more with the competition, you might use the following analogy: "It's like the difference between putting your own vacation together and paying for every extra cocktail or activity, and staying at an all-inclusive resort where everything's clear up front and you don't have to worry about any unpleasant surprises."

Simplify Your Slides.

Have you ever decided not to watch a movie on your iPad or that tiny airplane screen because you knew the size of the screen wouldn't do it justice? The same holds true for a virtual presentation. What works on the big screen doesn't always translate to the small screen. And, you have no idea how big (or small) your customer's screen is. Keep your graphics simple and crisp. And don't dawdle on them too long. If there is little to see on your slide, or once your customer has gotten what they need from it, you're much better off getting out of screen share and allowing your customer to connect with the full video image of you.

Practice Using Technology.

Poor execution or a lack of preparation may lead to lost time, lost attention, and confusion. Worse, it's easy for your prospect to associate a poorly executed video meeting with you, your company, or your product. Familiarize yourself with all of the tools that you're going to use well before that first call. As technology continues to improve, so will the expectations of your customers. You'll need to continue stepping up to the virtual plate so be prepared to use your tools as effectively as possible.

Managing Questions and Answers in Virtual Meetings

Many sellers say they want questions, yet don't have a plan for how and when they're going to answer them. This is quite dangerous, especially when you have a large audience. Like most presenters, you have a finite amount of time to get through your presentation, pitch, or demo, and still allow sufficient time for Q&A. You can't afford to get hijacked by audience members with ulterior motives or disruptive digital behavior. Here are some tips:

Set a Limited Q&A Time Prior to Your Closing.

If you have a tight agenda or more than a handful of people on the call, it's a good idea to take all but the most relevant questions just before the final recap of your meeting. This allows you to control the end of the meeting and avoid ending on a potentially negative question.

Let your audience know up front that you're going to take questions ten minutes before you close, for example. This cues your audience that you have set a time limit and helps keep earlier questions concise and on track. When you've hit the allotted time for Q&A, wrap up the question you're on, and move to your closing.

Stick to the Schedule.

Keeping your word is a crucial element of any relationship, and the end of the meeting is your opportunity to prove yourself to be trustworthy. If you promised that a meeting will end at a specified time, you need to honor that promise. Don't let one person hold the rest of the group hostage *(the only exception is if that one person is the boss!)*, or they will all end up resenting you. While this rule also applies to live presentations, it plays even greater importance virtually because people often leave less space between their meetings.

Manage your time and audience expectations by confirming the end time and explaining how you will be handling questions. When you are done, close at the designated time (or earlier), and if there are remaining questions, you can coordinate to take them off-line or schedule another call.

Go Full Camera During Q&A.

Throw out that slide with the giant question mark on it right now! In fact, get out of your slideware altogether during Q&A. There is no reason to compete with your slides for your audience's attention. The highest and best use of virtual real estate at the end of your meeting or call is to show your face. This is where you will cement the connection that you've created by looking your customer in the eye and answering their questions.

End Early.

I don't know anyone who doesn't love extra time back in their day. If you've covered all of your material and the Q&A has run its course, but there is still time left on the clock, don't fill it just because it's there. Inform your audience that you're going to end early. Trust me, they will be as happy as children who are let out of class before the bell!

Three Strategies for Dealing with Difficult Audience Members

On occasion, you may have someone in your video meeting or on your call whose sole mission seems to be to challenge you or throw you off track. Other times you may have people who are blissfully unaware that their behavior is disruptive or rude. In live meetings, these people would have often been managed by their peers or superiors.

Unfortunately, on a virtual call, participants can't see the disapproving looks or the eye rolls from others that might otherwise have discouraged their efforts. It's important to manage these people on video before they steal the show and sideline all of your hard work.

Following are three effective ways to deal with disruptive or difficult audience members:

1. **Park It.**
   When someone asks you a question that will either take you way off track or appears to be a set up for a debate, rein them in by parking their question. "Thanks for your question. We've got a number of topics to cover in our time today, so let me write that down, and we'll be certain to get back to it if we have time at the end of the call. If not, we can take it off-line." Following up this statement by writing down their question on a whiteboard or an open word document will often appease the asker by making them feel heard.

2. **Relay It.**
   You may have one individual who insists on monopolizing the conversation by peppering you with constant questions. If you let this person do all of the asking, the other participants often completely shut down. To open the conversation up to more people, pass the baton to another person on the call. For example, "Sarah brought up a good question. Jacob, how do you think this would work in your department?"

3. **Diffuse It.**
   Some people are born to run, and some are born to disagree. If a participant in your meeting disagrees with anything and everything you say, you need to take control of the situation early to avoid having their actions cast a pall on your entire meeting. Try diffusing the contrarian's position by letting them know that you value their opinion and that you want to know more about it outside of the presentation or meeting.

CHAPTER 12

STAYING CONNECTED WHEN USING NOTES, SLIDES, OR SCREENS

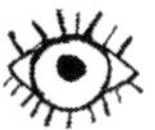

The best actors do not let the wheels show.

HENRY FONDA, ACTOR

Tyler worked for months to get an opportunity to present his solution to the entire buying committee of a Fortune 500 company. He was using two screens. The first screen held Tyler's camera, his platform panel and collaboration tools. The second screen had his PowerPoint deck and notes on it. Tyler started on screen one, greeting each individual on video as they arrived, and when he was ready to present, he turned his attention to the second screen.

After ten minutes, Tyler finally glanced back at his first screen only to notice a senior director had left early, but only after he'd posted a question in chat that Tyler missed. In addition, one person was clearly talking to someone off-camera and the remainder of the group had turned their cameras off.

This example is not uncommon, and you may even have experienced worse. It's easy to feel overwhelmed when you add more tasks to your virtual meeting, such as presenting slides or screens, accessing notes or a script, managing collaboration tools, and handling multiple people and multiple screens. How do you manage all of this and maintain a connection with your audience? It seems near impossible. Yet, it may be done with some preparation and know-how. But first, it's good to remember that there are a few things that hold true whether you are face-to-face or on video.

Three Rules for Using Scripts, Notes, or Slides on Video

1. **Don't Read from Your Slides.**

   It's a very poor customer experience when a presenter reads from their slides, whether live or on video. While many sellers have learned to rely less heavily on their slides when presenting face-to-face, this is far from the case on video. Even seasoned pros are apt to give in to temptation when the slides are right there under their nose. And it doesn't seem to matter whether there are two words on a slide or two hundred, presenters almost always have their eyes glued to their own slide, not the camera. So let me be clear: just because you're using slides on video does not grant you permission to read from them! As in a live presentation, you should be as familiar with your slides as possible.

2. **Don't Read from a Script.**

   There's a reason why actors like to have their lines memorized or be "off script" well before they get in front of the camera. It's difficult to focus on the meaning of the words or connecting with the other actors if they're still fumbling for lines. If the best of the best struggle to use a script easily, you can imagine what it sounds like when untrained professionals attempt to read from a script.

   Perhaps you don't have to imagine it. You may have been on a video call where the person is obviously reading from a script. The person's eyes move across the screen from left to right, their voice is stilted, and their natural inflection all but disappears. While this is more common on the phone, I see people doing the equivalent on video thinking they're getting away with it. They're not. Even on the phone, it is hard to pull off—but at least your customer's suspicions aren't confirmed by actually seeing you read from it with their own eyes!

I don't want to discourage you entirely from using a script, but a script or notes should only be used to serve one of three purposes on video (or the phone):

1. To organize your talking points
2. To use as an aid to memorization or achieving greater familiarity with your content
3. To have available to occasionally access specific information, get your bearings, or view upcoming topics during a video call

The first two methods are typically used for preparation and practice prior to a video meeting or recording, and the last is for use while you're in the meeting or doing the recording. Oftentimes, people use all three with the last one serving as a safety measure for those occasional blank spots. As you can see, there is no option for reading an entire script on video. Your audience can easily see (or hear) that you're reading which works against establishing authenticity and credibility.

To Memorize, or Not to Memorize?

Many salespeople tell me they don't want to memorize their pitch or presentation because they want it to be more conversational and they fear memorization will make it sound canned or phony. But... if memorization were the cause of bad line readings, people wouldn't shell out millions of dollars to watch actors in film, on television, and at the theater. Very few of these performances are unscripted. Memorization or practice is not the cause of poor performance either.

PRO TIP:

The canned type of delivery you fear has more to do with: A) Not investing the time necessary to put the script into your own words or: B) Improper rehearsal. The truth about memorizing your script is this: The better you know your script, the greater your ability to improvise off script.

Knowing your lines well enough that you don't have to search for words or meaning gives you confidence and frees you up to invest your energy on being present and responsive. Improvising or winging it entirely on video, where you have enough demands for your attention already, creates unnecessary stress. Under the best of circumstances, improvising tends to be wildly inconsistent. Knowing your pitch allows you to flow in and out of it as the conversation directs, while still maintaining enough control to get back to your main points.

So, am I proposing you memorize your script or presentation word-for-word? Not necessarily. While complete memorization works for some people, a great compromise is memorizing key lines and transition points for greater confidence and control. For example, I recommend always having the following elements committed to memory:

- **The First Line of Your Script or Presentation**
  The first words out of your mouth contribute to your audience's first impression of you. Why pressure yourself to think of something brilliant on the spot? As most actors can attest, nerves are always at the highest when the camera light goes on. But once the actor successfully delivers their first line their natural rhythm and practice kick in and their confidence returns.

- **The First Line of Every Slide or Topic**
  Do you enjoy writing copy on demand? If not, don't force yourself to write fresh material in your head every time a new slide appears. Set yourself up to succeed by deciding in advance the best way to frame each slide.

- **Transition Lines**
  The way transitions between slides and topics are handled is what separates the pros from the amateurs. Awkward or non-existent transitions can make the audience feel like a slide is as

much a surprise to you as it is to them. Always know how you're going to connect your current slide to the next one by coming up with a short entrance line for some of your more important or content-heavy slides. For example, "Now that we've talked about the challenges associated with the way you're currently collecting data, let's take a look at a solution." This allows for a much smoother transition and makes you appear more confident and knowledgeable.

- **The Last Line of Your Script or Presentation**
  If you don't know what your last line is, it's very easy to keep talking long after you've made your point. (Some salespeople have talked themselves right out of a sale by not knowing when to stop!) Know your last line and when you reach it, stop. Let the impact of what you've just said resonate with your listener and allow them a chance to respond.

- **All Key Lines**
  These are any lines that you A) don't want to forget or B) you don't want to get wrong. Value propositions, benefits, and metrics are examples of key lines in sales. Struggling to communicate your value proposition or transposing critical numbers can cause your prospect to doubt your credibility. Avoid that by having those key lines committed to heart.

3. **Maintain Eye Contact with Your Audience While Presenting**
   Maintaining a high level of quality eye contact with your audience when presenting is just as important on video—if not more—than face-to-face. It's very easy for your virtual audience to check out when they see that you are preoccupied with your slides or software. Of course, staying visually connected with your audience is more challenging on video because you are often managing additional inputs, like scripts, slides, notes, cameras, and platform tools. The following techniques will help simplify that process and

allow you to run your meeting, deliver an impactful message, and stay engaged with your audience as much as possible.

- **Position Your Script or Notes.**

  Place your notes or script in a spot that makes it easy for you to glance at them without making a huge leap with your eyes. If your notes are on-screen, either in a document or in PowerPoint presenter view, place them as close to the camera as possible. If you are using multiple screens and need frequent access to your notes or script, put them on the screen with your camera.

  If you're using printed notes, place them on a stand or easel just behind or to the side of your camera. If you only need a few bullet points to trigger your memory, I've found a physical whiteboard placed behind your camera also works well.

- **Accessing Your Script or Notes During a Presentation or Call**

  You may be wondering how it is possible to connect with your audience if you need to use a script or notes. The table read is a rehearsal technique used by professional actors when they first receive a script and want to begin rehearsing it before they have their lines committed to memory. The goal is to establish a connection with their scene partner while familiarizing themselves with their lines.

  If you want to see a fun example of a table read in action, check out the final table read for HBO's *Game of Thrones*. The entire cast received the last script three days before the table read, giving them time to familiarize themselves with their lines but not necessarily memorize them. When it came time to say their lines, most cast members would look down at the script to find their line, then look up and deliver their line to their scene partner in character.

BEHIND THE CAMERA

Fun GOT fact: Kit Harrington, aka, Jon Snow was the only actor who did not read the final script in advance. He stated that he didn't what to know what happened next. At the table read he was gasping and tearing up as the dramatic conclusion was revealed. He later admitted he didn't read the script because of laziness.

Even though the actors are not off-script, you can see the connections between the characters start to build. This would never happen if they were face down in their script. And it won't happen for you if you're face down in your script either.

- **Applying the Table Read Method**

Start by familiarizing yourself with your script or notes as much as possible. As an actor, I always read and re-read a script multiple times before a table read. If you're a visual person, read your script or presentation until you can picture approximately where a particular line or section is on the page or slide, even if you can't remember the exact words.

Once you are somewhat familiar with your script, practice the table read approach in front of your camera by looking into the camera and saying your first line *(you should always have your first line memorized!)*. Continue until you get to a place where you need to look at the script. Quickly glance down at your script and locate the line.

After you've located it, quickly look back at the camera and say your line as if you were talking to your customer. Say the full line to the camera. Try not to talk while you're looking at your notes. The goal is to re-establish eye contact with the camera first and then speak.

Run through this process a few times: when you need a line, locate it in your script, deliver it to the camera, and repeat. This will help familiarize you with your content as you practice, and in a live conversation it will allow you to maintain a connection with your customer and deliver your presentation with a more authentic intonation than if you were reading it straight from a script.

This process may seem a bit choppy initially, but once you become more familiar with your script, you'll be able to go right to the location you need, see one or two keywords that jog your memory, and go right back to the camera.

As you apply this in a live conversation, you may find yourself pausing longer than you usually do. This is not a bad thing. Remember, most people on video need to pause more and this may provide the needed brakes. Taking the time to connect with your audience by looking at the camera will have a much greater impact than delivering part of your message to your notes and part in mid-air.

- **Keeping Your Audience in the Loop**
  If you're unsure where the information you need is located in your notes or script and are concerned it might take you more than a few seconds to find it, simply alert your audience before you go searching for it. For example, say you asked me if I had any research on the effectiveness of using video in sales. I know I have that statistic but I'm not sure exactly where it is in my notes, so I might handle it as follows:

  (Looking at the camera) "That's a great question. I have a very interesting statistic about using video and sales. Let me find it for you so that I don't misquote it."

  (Break eye contact to search notes. Locate quote and silently read until get it in my head.)

  (Return to camera) "Yes, a study by Gong revealed that calls in which video was used were 41 percent more likely to result in a sale than calls when video was not used."

You can see that I followed the same process. I let my customer know what I was going to do, found the content, then brought my focus back to the camera to deliver it, all the while maintaining as much eye contact as possible with my customer.

Obviously, the quicker you can find what you need, the better. This is why part of your preparation is to familiarize yourself as much as possible with your supporting material so that you can quickly return your focus to your customer.

Leveraging Multiple Screens and or Cameras

There are few things more frustrating during virtual presentations than having to stare at the side of a presenter's head. It always looks to me like the presenter is talking to someone across the room. This is hardly conducive to creating a near in-person experience. Remember that while initially your audience's focus will be drawn to the content you're sharing, they will eventually look to your face and body language to provide context and meaning to what you've shared. That's very hard to do if they're presented with an image of only half of your face on their screen.

If you need to go back and forth between screens (like Tyler) and want to maintain that connection with your audience when you switch screens, I suggest using the Multiple Camera method mentioned in Chapter 4.

With two cameras (either an external webcam and the camera in your laptop or two external webcams) you control your audience's view and can keep them engaged during set changes just like a director of a television show.

Each screen should have a camera set up in as similar a frame as possible to avoid a jarring effect on your audience. (For example, you don't want one frame to be you in a medium close-up and the other to be you in an extreme close-up.) Choose the appropriate camera from the video controls in your platform or from a separate video switching device, like the ATEM Mini, whenever you move to the other screen. Here are some best practices for smoothly switching cameras and screens during a presentation:

- Avoid rapidly switching back and forth between screens or cameras. This draws unnecessary attention to the technique itself, overshadowing your message and connection.
- Switch cameras during natural transitions, like between slides or types of content, as opposed to mid-sentence.
- Ensure your microphone can pick you up clearly on both camera angles (with the ATEM Mini you can also alternate mics).
- Allow a few seconds to pass after you switch before you start talking from your new position.
- Practice switching from camera to camera and making eye contact with each camera. If you're used to one camera, you will need to learn to quickly "hit your mark," i.e., locate the camera lens with your eyes. Remember, there's no sense in doing multiple cameras if you're not going to look at them!

Using a Producer to Manage Your Meeting

Managing the many inputs available to you when running virtual meetings or presentations can feel a lot like putting on a one-person show. Juggling your platform, your participants, your content, while trying to read body language and take notes leaves lots of room for errors and missed signals. The questions and cues that Tyler missed could likely have been avoided entirely if he'd had a producer.

A producer is typically a team member or support staff who joins the meeting to monitor some of these channels, freeing you up to focus on connecting with your audience and getting your message across.

Before you grab your best buddy to be your producer, determine what precisely you'd like your producer to do. If you want them to manage technical issues, upload polls, and run breakout rooms, you may want a producer who's more technically savvy than if you simply want someone to read and alert you to changes in body language, and or take notes. Often salespeople make a quid pro quo arrangement with another seller to support each other on their more important calls. This has the added benefit of allowing you to become familiar with each other's styles and rhythm and keep learning and improving as you go.

Below are some guidelines for working with your producer before, during, and after your session to achieve the best possible outcome.

PRE-SESSION:

- **Clearly define duties.** Determine who will let participants into the meeting, monitor chat or questions, take notes, read body language set up breakout rooms, etc.
- **Specify when to take action.** Let your producer know what you would like them to look for and what and when they should take action. For example, what body language signals should they alert you to? What types of questions or comments do you want to address right away? Which can wait?
- **Establish a back channel.** How will you and your producer communicate during the meeting? Chat? Text? DM? *(I recommend using an alternative to the platform chat as it's too easy to slip up and send messages to the entire group.)*
- **Provide your producer with a script.** Outline the flow of the meeting, including what content is to be shared and when, transitions, and section timing to eliminate unpleasant surprises and awkward gaps.
- **Do a tech rehearsal.** Run through all the tools you're going to use (chat, polls, annotations, screen sharing, etc.) as well as each transition in your presentation, since that's where many errors and lags occur.

DURING SESSION:

- **Join early to upload all content and test your platform, audio/ video, tools, annotations, and polls.**
- **Allow participants into the meeting.**
- **Record or take notes.**
- **Manage technical support.**
- **Monitor chat.**
- **Do time checks.**
- **Check body language.**
- **Start/stop polls.**
- **Run breakout rooms.**

POST SESSION:

- **Do a debrief offline.** Never discuss your meeting in the same room, lest participants still be online. Set up a new session or jump on a call.
- **Discuss observations.** You both have a different perspective during the meeting, so it's valuable to hear each person's impressions of both the overall engagement and receptivity level, as well as that of individual members.
- **Exchange notes or the recording.**
- **Provide constructive feedback.** What went well? What could have gone better?
- **Make a list of specific improvements to make for the next session.**

Smoothing Out Rocky Transitions

Transitions between screens, slides, and full video are where presenters tend to lose a percentage of their audience on video. Watching you struggle to locate your content, share your screen, or switch screens, provides them an easy opportunity to minimize you and check out one of their other open windows.

One salesperson had her audience on the edge of their seats, excited to watch a video demonstration that she had been touting, but when she hit play, there was no video or sound. She clicked around for a minute and the video finally appeared, but there was still no sound. After an excruciating few minutes of searching and fielding suggestions from the audience (always a feel-good moment for presenters!), she gave up and she did her best to provide her own play-by-play of the video. Needless to say, it was a bit anti-climactic for all. Only later did she learn about a setting in her platform that needed to be turned on in order to share sound and video with her audience.

Here are some tips to avoid these momentum-killers and ensure your audience stays engaged throughout your presentation or demonstration:

- **Familiarize yourself with how to share various types of content on your platform. This will avoid a lot of unnecessary fumbling around.**
- **Have your content open ahead of time to eliminate the extra steps required to locate the desired document or app for sharing.**
- **Close all of the screens and programs that you're not using during your call.** It is an unwritten law that the screen you want to share will be at the very end of your list. If you have fifty other programs or screens open, you may get anxious if you don't see the needed screen right away. Give yourself some peace of mind and have open only what you need to show and nothing else.
- **When given a choice between sharing your desktop or an app, share the app.** I have seen a number of items that I am quite confident the presenter would have preferred I did not see! If you are using your web browser, make sure you go full screen for the same reason.

How to Talk to your Audience During Transitions

Moving between slides or screens can be awkward if there is a lag or if you're transitioning between different types of content. Many sellers feel the need to provide a blow-by-blow explanation of what they are doing behind the scenes. This can be both unnecessary and distracting for you and your audience. My advice? Keep it to yourself unless the lag is unusually long.

By now, your audience should be familiar with what takes place when a screen is shared. They likely know from firsthand experience that it may take a few seconds for you to find your content. And they're probably aware that it might take another few seconds for your content to appear on their screen. Unless your screen share takes an unusually long time to load, it's perfectly acceptable to pause in silence for up to ten to fifteen seconds and focus on getting your content on the screen.

If you happen to be good at multi-tasking, you can talk about what the audience will see, but please don't tell the audience every issue you're having along the way. In other words, just do it! Below are some more behind-the-scenes items that your audience does not need to be privy to, and what to do or say instead:

- **When you locate your file or screen:** Don't exclaim, *"Aha! There it is."* This makes your customer wonder why you are surprised. *Have you not done this before? Did you forget that we had this meeting scheduled?* Instead, just show it.
- **When you share your screen:** There's no need to alert your customer by saying, "We should see it in a moment." Instead, pause long enough to let the screen appear and ask them if they can see what is on your screen.
- **When you change slides:** It's unnecessary to announce, "I'm going to go to the next slide." Your customer is familiar with the process of moving from slide to slide. Instead, use that time to promote what they will be seeing or summarize what they've just seen.

PRO TIP:

Since no one but you knows what's on your screen, be specific., e.g., "Can you see the graph on your screen?"

CHAPTER 13

BECOMING YOUR OWN DIRECTOR

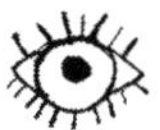

I feel I have to work hard to nurture whatever talent I have as an actor. I feel like it's not natural to me. So I don't take it for granted.

DAVID DUCHOVNY, ACTOR/DIRECTOR

You've seen by now that there is a lot more to building a relationship on video than turning on your camera. So now you may be thinking, how do I start?

Well, I can tell you how *not* to start: Don't try to do everything at once, and don't start by practicing on high-stakes calls. One of my clients became so rattled and self-conscious trying to make direct eye contact, stay within frame, and speak with variety on a video call with an important customer that they forgot to share their PowerPoint. About ten minutes into the call the customer politely inquired, "Am I supposed to be seeing something on my screen?"

Here is my recommended approach for putting all you've learned into action. If you haven't done the exercises included at the end of each chapter, I suggest you go back and start there before moving on. Once you're done, you're ready to launch into the Ten Steps outlined below, which, like the earlier exercises, includes recording and reviewing yourself. If your reaction is, no thanks, I'd rather stick a needle in my eye than watch myself on video; you're in good company. Many people feel that way, even actors who spend a lot of time on camera.

BEHIND THE CAMERA

Adam Driver made headlines for walking out of an NPR podcast interview after host Terry Gross wanted to play a clip of him singing in his film, *A Marriage Story.* The actor famously hates listening to or watching himself in his own movies, saying "I drive myself and the other people around me crazy with the things I wanted to change."

About seeing himself on screen, Zac Efron said, "I tend to...pick out every single flaw, or things I could have and should have done better."

Yes, You Have to Watch Your Own Video to Improve.

Famous actors may be able to get away without reviewing their work, but only because they have directors to offer them objective feedback and guidance. The rest of us can't afford to be in the dark about what our audience is seeing and experiencing on their screen. Our options are to either enlist a colleague, coach, or manager to review our videos and provide feedback, or to do it ourselves. Either way, this step is vital as it allows for critical insights that may help you connect and communicate more successfully with your audience. Without feedback, many people fall back on old and ineffective behaviors on video.

Asking Others for Feedback

Having someone else provide feedback on your performance can be highly enlightening. Others are, by definition, more objective and able to pick up behaviors that may exist in our blind spot. On the other hand, opening yourself up to feedback is a vulnerable experience so choose your partner wisely.

Whether a colleague, a trusted friend, or a coach, look for someone who can be honest, constructive, and kind. Choose someone whose good opinion you're not afraid to lose if your performance is less than perfect. This individual doesn't necessarily need to be great on video themselves—but they should know what "good" looks like. Generally, an independent coach or a peer who is also working on improving their own video skills is best suited for this role.

Let your partner know precisely what you want them to focus on. I recommend using an evaluation checklist to help your partner focus on specific areas. You can find one that I use on my website: juliehansen.live.

Be aware that without clear direction, it's easy for co-workers or managers to veer off into a discussion of the best way to show a feature, or wordsmith a certain point. While valuable, feedback on your content or messaging may keep you from focusing on the main objective: successfully connecting with your audience on video. Have your partner set aside any notes regarding content or messaging for a separate conversation.

When ready, ask your partner to read the "What a Good Director Does (and Doesn't) Do" section below for guidance on how to give specific and constructive feedback. Then follow the first four steps in the "Ten Steps to Direct Your Video Performance" below with your partner.

What a Good Director Does (and Doesn't) Do

If you're invested in your career, you need to learn how to review yourself on video objectively and constructively. Unfortunately, those two words, objective and constructive, may not be the first two words that come to mind when watching your own video performance!

Even as an actor I hated watching myself on video for a few years. All I could see were the flaws: I didn't smile enough. My voice sounded flat. I blinked too much; The list went on and on. All this self-awareness only served to make me more anxious and self-conscious the next time I was in front of the camera.

It wasn't until I shifted my perspective from that of a performer to a director that I was able to review my recordings constructively and use them as a tool to improve instead of a stick to beat myself up with. You can also learn to adopt a good director's perspective by first understanding what a good director does and does not do.

A good director does:

- Ensure you have enough time to prepare
- Provide honest, direct feedback in a kind and respectful manner
- Encourage and acknowledge what works
- Eliminate tension on the set, allowing for necessary physical and mental breaks
- Offer specific suggestions that will improve the audience's understanding, engagement, or interest

A good director does NOT:

- Provide only negative feedback
- Shame you for hereditary traits, physical limitations, or mannerisms you've developed over years of presenting face-to-face
- Care about what you meant to do
- Expect you to change everything at once
- Leave you on your own to figure out what's needed to improve

If you've been a bad director to yourself until now, it's time to put on the good director's hat and look at your performance strictly from a what worked/what didn't standpoint with no shame and no blame. This approach takes much of the sting out of feedback and allows you to focus on specific solutions rather than getting stuck in a generalized sense of not being good enough.

The following ten steps walk you through how to review a recent video call or meeting and take action in a logical and constructive way.

Ten Steps to Direct Your Own Video Performance

1. **Review your video for what you did well.** I know you want to pick out all the things you're doing wrong but resist that urge. Directors give a fair and balanced report so take a moment to write down what you did well before you get lost in the weeds. Everyone does something well on video. What are your strengths? Where did you shine, even if just for a moment? Perhaps your eye contact was strong at the beginning and end of the call. Maybe your lighting really made your face and eyes pop. Write it all down.
2. **Review your video for improvement.** Even though I asked you to watch your video for what you did well, I bet you couldn't help but notice a few (or more?) areas where you might need some improvement. For example, it could be that you're not making nearly enough direct eye contact, your gestures are unclear, or your face veers towards RBF.
3. **Pick one specific area to work on that will have the most immediate impact on your ability to connect with your audience.** For many people, this is making better eye contact or eliminating distracting movements, like jutting their head toward the camera. Select just one of these areas to work on initially and set the rest of your list aside for now.
4. **Watch your video again and place your focus on this single area.** As you review the video, get granular about what you're currently doing and why. For example, if your focus area is making better eye contact, perhaps you observe that you are getting stuck looking at the screen when your customer speaks, or you're relying too heavily on your slides.
5. **Review the corresponding chapter in this book that addresses your area of focus for anything you may have overlooked.** Run through the exercises again. For example, if you want to improve your eye contact, review the steps and exercises for making

good, direct eye contact with your customer in Chapter 5.

6. **Develop a specific action plan.** Awareness is great, but if you don't turn it into action you're not going to see any results. Brainstorm all the ways you could improve in your focus area. For example, if you are working on being more expressive, you could do the facial muscle warm-ups in Chapter 9 before each call. You could ensure you're in a passionate high-energy state before each call by focusing on what's at stake for your customer. You could catch yourself when you think you're smiling and quickly check a mirror to see if your smile is visible on screen.
7. **Do a practice session on video.** Turn on your video and try your skills out during a mock presentation or conversation. Practice first with your image visible (so you can check in real time) and when you feel like you've developed some muscle memory with the skill, try it again with your image hidden. While you don't want to let go of any other good video skills you've developed, give yourself permission to focus on practicing this one skill.
8. **Practice on low-stakes calls.** Don't try out your new skills on a high-stakes call right away or you might end up like my client—so focused on the skill you forget about the customer! Calls with friends, family, or colleagues are great low-risk ways to practice new techniques.
9. **Record yourself.** Once you've practiced the skill a few times, both on your own and on low-risk calls, record yourself. Compare this recording to your initial video, note (and perhaps celebrate) where you've improved. If there's still work to be done, that's normal. Old habits are rarely broken in a few days. Keep fine-tuning, and when you feel like you're close to mastering that skill, go on to the next one on your list.

10. **Access additional tools or resources that may help you.** Many people still find it difficult to be objective or to coach themselves to improve. Some people have well-worn habits or behaviors that are especially resistant to change. In that case, below are some resources that you may find useful.
11. **Bonus Step: Re-take the Test at the end of Chapter 2 and compare your new results to your original results.** Did you see a 25% or more increase in the amount of eye contact you're making with your audience? Keep at it until you get to that 80% mark.

You'll find numerous video tips, articles, and tools available at juliehansen.live to support your efforts to improve your video skillset.

The Selling On-Video Master Class, also at juliehansen.live, is a self-paced video course where I demonstrate many of the techniques and exercises in this book as well as guide you to practice them and apply them. There's also additional coaching and virtual workshops to help you improve quickly.

MANAGER'S TIP:

If you'd like to use your newfound knowledge to coach your team, having them go through the video course first will make your coaching efforts a whole lot easier and more effective. This provides everyone with a common language and a set of actions to measure.

The Journey Continues

I encourage you to continue to record yourself at least monthly, identifying where you need more polish. Work on those areas one at a time—both on and off camera. After a few months, compare your most recent recording to the one you did at the start of this journey. If you're like most people, you'll see a dramatic improvement in your virtual presence and your ability to draw your audience in and make them feel seen, heard, and engaged. You'll find that you are able to express authenticity, attentiveness, interest, empathy, and credibility clearly on video. No longer will your customers, partners, or team members wonder whether you're interested in them or reading an email. No more will you panic at the sight of a blank face—or no face—on video.

While others continue to struggle to get relationships off the ground on video, you will be miles ahead, building meaningful relationships that lead to more sales, improved collaboration, and greater productivity. You have developed an awareness around the verbal and nonverbal messages you're sending on video and the muscle memory to communicate with confidence. You are ready to meet the communication challenges of this moment, and tomorrow's moments, head on, looking your audience in the eye!

And that my friends, as they say on set, is "Scene."

ABOUT THE AUTHOR

Lights, camera, action! Julie Hansen has walked in the shoes of sellers, leaders, and on-camera professionals.

A recognized thought-leader on video communications and presentations, Julie is the author of two other sales books, *Sales Presentations for Dummies* and *ACT Like a Sales Pro! How to Command the Business Stage and Dramatically Increase Your Sales with Proven Acting Techniques.*

In addition to a career in sales and leadership, Julie worked in front of the camera as a professional actor, appearing in over 50 commercials, films, and television shows, including HBO's *Sex & The City.* In her Selling on Video Master Class Julie marries her experience and insights from sales and performance to help non-actors communicate and connect more successfully on video.

Julie Hansen resides in Denver, Colorado. For more information on Julie's keynotes and video workshops for your organization, email julie@actingforsales. For the latest video tips and tricks, visit juliehansen.live.

ACKNOWLEDGMENTS

First and foremost, my heartfelt gratitude to my husband Beau, who barely flinched when I told him I was writing a third book. Thank you for cheering me on while taking on more than your fair share of home maintenance during this project.

Thank you to Alice Heiman for "nudging" me into writing this book and to everyone in my Master Mind Group for keeping me squarely on the path.

A shout out to Lisa Dennis, who captured my vision so clearly in the title; to Molly Gibson, who patiently helped me vet hundreds of candidates; and Doug Eymer, responsible for the book design and the perfect eye-catching cover.

To my dear friend and talented artist, Becky Laschanzky, thank you for sharing your trade secrets so we may all look our best and feel more confident on camera.

Thank you to television pros Jenn Mueller and Joel Goldberg for sharing insights from their careers on camera. And to the many hard-working screen actors, directors, and on-camera coaches from whom I've been fortunate enough to learn, your techniques, tips, and tricks have never been more widely needed!

A single set of eyes on a book is never enough, so thank goodness for Peter Cohan and Steffen Sajonz. This book is tighter and has fewer mixed metaphors because of their efforts.

Finally, I couldn't have done this without the many salespeople, business leaders, and entrepreneurs who realized that turning on the camera was just the beginning of the journey to connect. Through our work together you inspired and challenged me to make every suggestion actionable and practical to meet the realities of conducting business virtually, like back-to-back meetings, clients not being on-camera, and multiple inputs fighting for your attention. Your experiences have informed this book and made it more relevant for those who follow in your footsteps.

ENDNOTES

[i] Andris A. Zoltners, Pk Sinha, and Sally E. Lorimer. "How to Reach New Customers When You Can't Meet Them in Person," *Harvard Business Review*, January, 13, 2021, https://hbr.org/2021/01/how-to-reach-new-customers-when-you-cant-meet-them-in-person.

[ii] "Sales Transformation Strategies: The Future of Sales." Gartner, accessed June 21, 2021, https://www.gartner.com/en/sales/trends/future-of-sales.

[iii] Paul J. Zak, "The Neuro-Science of Trust." *Harvard Business Review*. (Jan-Feb. 2017) https://hbr.org/2017/01/the-neuroscience-of-trust

[iv] Sue Carter, "The Role of Oxytocin and Vasopressin in Attachment," *Psychodynamic Psychiatry*, December, 2017 Vol. 45 (4), pp.499-517.

[v] Allan Pease. "Body language, the power is in the palm of your hands." TEDx Macquarie University (Nov. 7, 2013) https://www.youtube.com/watch?v=ZZZ7k8cMA-4

[vi] John R. DiJulius III, Joel Richards, et al. *The Relationship Economy: Building Stronger Customer Connections in the Digital Age* (Austin, TX: Greenleaf Book Group Press, 2019).

[vii] Helene Kreysa, Luise Kessler, and Stefan R. Schweinberger. "Direct Speaker Gaze Promotes Trust in Truth-Ambiguous Statements." *PLOS ONE* 11, no. 9 (September 19, 2016). https://doi.org/10.1371/journal.pone.0162291.

[vii] Allan Pease. "Body language, the power is in the palm of your hands."

[ix] Nalini Ambady and Robert Rosenthal. "Half a Minute: Predicting Teacher Evaluations from Thin Slides of Nonverbal Behavior and Physical Attractiveness," *Journal of Personality and Social Psychology* 67, no. 3 (1993): 431-44. https://psycnet.apa.org/record/1993-27364-001

[x] Shu Morioka, Michihiro Osumi, Mayu Shiotani, Satoshi Nobusako, Hiroshi Maeoka, Yohei Okada, Makoto Hiyamizu, and Atsushi Matsuo. "Incongruence between Verbal and Non-Verbal Information Enhances the Late Positive Potential." *PLOS ONE* 11, no. 10 (October 13, 2016). https://doi.org/10.1371/journal.pone.0164633.

[xi] "Communication Loop / The Process of Communication." Communication Theory, July 10, 2014. https://www.communicationtheory.org/communication-loop-the-process-of-communication/

[xii] Casey Chan. "How Different Camera Lenses Can Make You Look Fatter." Gizmodo, September 4, 2018. https://gizmodo.com/watch-how-different-camera-lenses-can-make-you-look-fat-1784458991.

[xiii] Hiromi Kobayashi and Shiro Kohshima. "Unique Morphology of the Human Eye and Its Adaptive Meaning: Comparative Studies on External Morphology of the Primate Eye." *Journal of Human Evolution* 40, no. 5 (May 2001): 419–35. https://doi.org/10.1006/jhev.2001.0468.

[xiv] Cohen, Lola. *The Lee Strasberg Notes*. (Routledge 2010), pgs. 13-17.

[xv] Michelle Jarick and Alan Kingstone. "The Duality of Gaze: Eyes Extract and Signal Social Information during Sustained Cooperative and Competitive Dyadic Gaze." *Frontiers in Psychology* 6 (September 23, 2015). https://doi.org/10.3389/fpsyg.2015.01423.

[xvi] Jodi Schulz. "Eye Contact: Don't Make These Mistakes." MSU Extension, December 31, 2012. https://www.canr.msu.edu/news/eye_contact_dont_make_these_mistakes.

[xvii] Jefferson Graham. "Ready for Your Zoom: What's the Best Camera for Video Meetings?" USA Today. Gannett Satellite Information Network, September 22, 2020. https://www.usatoday.com/story/tech/2020/09/22/zoom-tips-how-look-great-best-camera-webcam-iphone/3476930001/.

[xviii] *Psychology Today* Staff. "First Impressions." Psychology Today. Sussex Publishers, 2021. https://www.psychologytoday.com/us/basics/first-impressions.

[xix] Nina Brown. (2001). Edward T. Hall, Proxemic Theory, 1966. *CSISS Classics. UC Santa Barbara: Center for Spatially Integrated Social Science.* Retrieved from https://escholarship.org/uc/item/4774h1rm

[xx] Amanda Erickson. "What 'Personal Space' Looks Like around the World." *The Washington Post.* April 24, 2017. https://www.washingtonpost.com/news/worldviews/wp/2017/04/24/how-close-is-too-close-depends-on-where-you-live/

[xxi] Dennis. "Podcast Mic Techniques For New Hosts (11 Important Tips)." Castos, May 12, 2020. https://castos.com/mic-techniques/

[xxii] MasterClass Staff. "How Breaking the Fourth Wall Works in Film and TV - 2021." MasterClass. MasterClass, November 8, 2020. https://www.masterclass.com/articles/how-breaking-the-fourth-wall-works-in-film-and-tv#what-is-the-fourth-wall.

[xxiii] Bojana Kuzmanovic, Alexandra L. Georgescu, Simon B. Eickhoff, Nadim J. Shah, Gary Bente, Gereon R. Fink, and Kai Vogeley. "Duration Matters: Dissociating Neural Correlates of Detection and Evaluation of Social Gaze." *NeuroImage* 46, no. 4 (July 15, 2009): 1154–63. https://doi.org/10.1016/j.neuroimage.2009.03.037.

[xxiv] Rick Walters. TCU Magazine. Accessed June 21, 2021. http://www.magarchive.tcu.edu/articles/2005-01-AC2.asp.

[xxv] Kuzmanovic, et al. "Duration Matters: Dissociating Neural Correlates of Detection and Evaluation of Social Gaze." NeuroImage 46, no. 4 (July 15, 2009): 1154–63. https://doi.org/10.1016/j.neuroimage.2009.03.037.

[xxvi] Kuzmanovic, et al. "Duration Matters: Dissociating Neural Correlates of Detection and Evaluation of Social Gaze." NeuroImage 46, no. 4 (July 15, 2009): 1154–63. https://doi.org/10.1016/j.neuroimage.2009.03.037.

[xxvii] Gillian Aeria. "Why We Show the Whites of Our Eyes." The University of Melbourne. October 21, 2016. https://pursuit.unimelb.edu.au/articles/why-we-show-the-whites-of-our-eyes

[xxviii] Quiroga, R. Quian, L. Reddy, G. Kreiman, C. Koch, and I. Fried. "Invariant Visual Representation by Single Neurons in the Human Brain." *Nature* 435, no. 7045 (2005): 1102–7. https://doi.org/10.1038/nature03687.

[xxix] Aaron Sorkin. *A Few Good Men.* The Internet Movie Script Data Base. Revised Third Draft, July 15, 1991. https://imsdb.com/scripts/A-Few-Good-Men.html

[xxx] Tomas Chamorro-Premuzic. "Why Being Predictable Is Actually a Great Thing According to Science." Fast Company, December 20, 2019. https://www.fastcompany.com/90444591 why-being-predictable-is-actually-a-great-thing-according-to-science.

[xxxi] Margaret Mercedes Mccarthy. "SiOWfa14 Science in Our World: Certainty and Cont." SiOWfa14 Science in Our World Certainty and Cont, October 24, 2014. https://sites.psu.edu/siowfa14/2014/10/21/is-smiling-contagious/.

[xxxii] Hans Strasburger, Ingo Rentschler, and Martin Juttner. "Peripheral Vision and Pattern Recognition: A Review." *Journal of Vision* 11, no. 5 (December 2011): 13–13. https://doi.org/10.1167/11.5.13.

[xxxiii] Roxanne Bauer. "The Impact of Making Eye Contact around the World." World Economic Forum, February 26, 2015. https://www.weforum.org/agenda/2015/02/the-impact-of-making-eye-contact-around-the-world/.

[xxxiv] Carol Kinsey Goman. "To Read Body Language Like a Pro, Look for Clusters." BBN Times, March 31, 2018. https://www.bbntimes.com/companies/to-read-body-language-like-a-pro-look-for-clusters.

[xxxv] Allan and Barbara Pease. "'The Definitive Book of Body Language'." The New York Times, September 24, 2006. https://www.nytimes.com/2006/09/24/books/chapters/0924-1st-peas.html.

[xxxvi] Carol Kinsey Goman. "Great Leaders Talk With Their Hands." *Forbes Magazine*, September 21, 2010. https://www.forbes.com/2010/09/21/body-language-hands-gestures-forbes-woman-leadership-communication.html?sh=77a68be628bc.

[xxxvii] Kris Konrath. "The Human Brain: Hardwired for Motion." Blog by Convergent, April 6, 2017. https://www.convergent.com/resources/the-human-brain-hardwired-for-motion/.

[xxxviii] Simon Worrall. "You Need Your Personal Space-Here's the Science Why." *National Geographic*, January 19, 2018.
https://www.nationalgeographic.com/science/article/personal-space-between-us-graziano-peripersonal-dyspraxia.

[xxxix] Robin McKie. "Psychology of Smiling: Can You Tell a Fake Smile from a Genuine One?" *The Guardian*. Guardian News and Media, April 10, 2015.
https://www.theguardian.com/science/2015/apr/10/psychology-empathy-distinguish-fake-genuine-smiles.

[xl] Caroline Burke. "This Is Why Smiling Is So Freaking Contagious, According To Science." *Elite Daily*, June 11, 2018. https://www.elitedaily.com/p/is-smiling-really-contagious-it-totally-is-the-science-behind-the-phenomenon-is-fascinating-9363923.

[xli] Robert F. Potter, Edgar J. Jamison-Koenig, Teresa Lynch, and Joshua Sites. "Effect of Vocal-Pitch Difference on Automatic Attention to Voice Changes in Audio Messages." *Communication Research* 46, no. 7 (December 2016): 1008–25. https://doi.org/10.1177/0093650215623835.

[xlii] Chris Orlob. "Data-Backed Sales Demo Tips to Help You Sell." Gong, September 14, 2017. https://www.gong.io/blog/sales-demos/.

[xliii] Chuck Murphy. The Shrinking Attention Span & What It Means for Marketers, August 27, 2017. https://www.bostondigital.com/insights/shrinking-attention-span-what-it-means-marketers#:~:text=In%20fact%2C%20a%20study%20by,an%20answer%20fast%20and%20easy.

[xliv] Mark P. Mattson. "Superior Pattern Processing Is the Essence of the Evolved Human Brain." *Frontiers in Neuroscience* 8 (August 22, 2014). https://doi.org/10.3389/fnins.2014.00265.

[xlv] Anne Fisher. "Giving a Speech? Conquer the Five-Minute Attention Span." *Fortune*, July 10, 2013. https://fortune.com/2013/07/10/giving-a-speech-conquer-the-five-minute-attention-span/.

[xlvi] Eric Jaffe. "Mirror Neurons: How We Reflect on Behavior." Association for Psychological Science - APS, May 1, 2007. https://www.psychologicalscience.org/observer/mirror-neurons-how-we-reflect-on-behavior.

[xlvii] Paul J Zak. "How Stories Change the Brain." *Greater Good Magazine*, December 17, 2017. https://greatergood.berkeley.edu/article/item/how_stories_change_brain.

Made in USA - Crawfordsville, IN
85343_9781737503705
04.10.2023 1855